AF497492

The
Smokeless Fire

Unravelling the secrets of
Isha, Kena & Katha Upanishads

Uttara Nerurkar

The Smokeless Fire

Unravelling the secrets of
Isha, Kena & Katha Upanishads

Uttara Nerurkar

B.Tech., Indian Institute of Technology, Kanpur
Vaidika Scholar
Previously a Software Researcher

ZEN
PUBLICATIONS
A Division of Maoli Media Private Limited

Dedicated to my father,

Shri Vinod Chandra Gupta, for gently and

lovingly putting me on the right path.

उत्तराहमुत्तर उत्तरेदुत्तराभ्यः ।
अथा सपत्नी या ममाधरा साधराभ्यः ॥ ऋग्वेद १०।१४५।३॥

O most excellent of elixirs, Soma! I, Upanishad, who am spiritual knowledge personified, am the best for the upliftment of human beings. In fact, I am the better than the best. And my enemy, worldly lust, is way below me. In fact, it is lower than the lowest.

The Smokeless Fire: Unravelling the secrets of Isha, Kena and Katha Upanishads

Copyright © 2018 Uttara Nerurkar

First Edition: November 2018

PUBLISHED BY
ZEN PUBLICATIONS
A Division of Maoli Media Private Limited
60, Juhu Supreme Shopping Centre,
Gulmohar Cross Road No. 9, JVPD Scheme,
Juhu, Mumbai 400 049. India.
Tel: +91 9022208074
eMail: info@zenpublications.com
Website: www.zenpublications.com

COVER & BOOK DESIGN
Red Sky Designs, Mumbai

ISBN 978-93-87242-21-0

CONTENTS

Preface   *8*

Acknowledgements   *10*

Introduction   *12*

THE WORD OF GOD: ISHOPANISHAD

Introduction to Ishopanishad   25

Ishopanishad: The Realm of the Lord   27

GRASPING THE UNKNOWN: KENOPANISHAD

Introduction to Kenopanishad   51

Section 1: The Hidden Motivator   52

Section 2: The Conundrum that is God   59

Section 3: The Parable of the Devas and Brahma   63

Section 4: The Parable Decoded   66

DEATH AND THE BOY: KATHOPANISHAD

Introduction to Kathopanishad   77

Chapter 1: At Death's Door   79

    Section I: Nachiketaa Meets Yama   79

    Section II: The Two Paths in Life   101

    Section III: Finding The Ultimate   121

Chapter 2: God and the Soul   137

    Section I: The Nature of God   137

    Section II: The Soul   149

    Section III: The Tree of the World   161

About the Author   *176*

*C*ontinuing from my earlier work, *The Causeless Cause: The Eternal Wisdom of Shwetaashwatara Upanishad,* a commentary on the Shwetaashwatara Upanishad, this book contains three of the most loved Upanishads – Isha, Kena and Katha. Considered the first three Upanishads, they are often read together.

The commentary follows the same style that the readers have come to expect, i.e., it presumes no prior knowledge whatsoever from the reader of the Vedas, the Upanishads, or Indian spiritual tenets in general. Also, it is brief and lucid, while not taking away from the depth of meaning of the Upanishad. It is, thus, written keeping the busy first-timer in mind.

Unlike other Upanishads that are from the Braahmanas or the Aaranyakas (ancient commentaries on the Vedas), Ishopanishad is directly from the Vedas. However, there is a slight difference between the Vaidika version and the Upanishadic one. This book covers both the versions, taking up the Vaidika one first, followed by the Upanishadic one. Being a chapter from the Yajurveda, this Upanishad is as authoritative as it gets. For this reason, it is considered first among Upanishads. This divine Upanishad covers a lot of ground – from the mundane duties of the Material world to the quest for spiritual salvation. Also, being part of a Veda, its language constructs are very unique. Mandatorily, Vedas should be interpreted by Rshis, or seers. For this reason, my commentary is based on the greatest seer of modern times, Swamee Dayaananda Saraswatee of the Arya Samaj.

Kenopanishad is a short, but oft-quoted Upanishad. It contains an endearing parable that places the Vedas as the fountainhead of all knowledge.

No-one needs an introduction to Kathopanishad! In some way or the other, the story of Yama and the boy Nachiketaa has percolated to each and every Indian. Its closeness to the Bhagawad Geeta has only added to its charm for its readers. The pull of the senses and the need to break away from them in order to achieve the ultimate goal of a human being forms the main theme of this Upanishad.

There being many layers of meaning in such texts, the new reader is strongly advised to read the Introduction before venturing forth into the Upanishad. This will provide the necessary grounding in Vaidika precepts.

I am confident the reader will be transported to a different sphere by each Upanishad and will leave her/him much enriched. I wish you an exciting journey of discovery and look forward to your reactions to these sublime Upanishads!

Uttara Nerurkar
Bangalore

November 21, 2018

ACKNOWLEDGEMENTS

The Kathopanishad was one of the earliest Upanishads taught to me by my father, Shri Vinod Chandra Gupta, in my teenage years. I did not comprehend its purport fully at the time. But over the years, with some experience of the world behind me, the message has become increasingly clear to me. As I lay this work at the feet of the Divine, I am also thankful for His sending my first teacher in the form of my father, who lovingly introduced me to so many scriptures. I pray that the Almighty grant my father an enlightened next life!

My devout mother always impressed me with her unflinching devotion to God and her simple but effective ethics. I pray that she live long, healthy and happy, spreading her cheer to those around her!

I am thankful to my students, past and present, who have always supported and embellished my enterprise. Each one of them is responsible for this work to some extent. I pray for their health, happiness and enlightenment!

My dear friends, Divya and Mrunalini, did a thorough check of the content and language of this work. I am deeply indebted to them and wish them many active years ahead!

I had a great association with publishers Zen Publications for my first book and I am happy to continue that relationship with this, my second book, as well.

I can never fully express my gratitude for my husband, who has always strongly supported every endeavour of mine. I pray for a beautiful and fulfilling life for him!

Finally I am thankful to all you dear readers for inspiring this second book. I hope you enjoy this work, too!

Om Shriparamaatmane Namah!

Introduction

The Upanishads

The Upanishads lie at the very core of ancient Indian spiritual thought. They are highly revered by Indians and the rest of the world alike. They contain answers to the deepest mystical questions that have troubled man since the beginning of time. They delve into the mysteries of the nature of this Universe, its purpose, the entities that inhabit it, the relationship between them – particularly between God and the individual soul – and the ultimate goal of life. The last is really the *raison d'être* of every Upanishad – how to release the spirit from worldly encumbrances and provide it salvation. Sometimes, they also cover the right way to live this worldly life, i.e., the path of Dharma. Due to their esoteric subject matter, they are considered a subordinate part, or Upaangas, of the Vedas – the supreme revered books of the Hindus. Some even call them 'the essence of the Vedas', although this epithet may not be entirely justified.

Their antiquity can only be guessed as they were written sometime in the Vaidika era, which itself is variously dated by scholars from 2500 to 5000 years ago, but is considerably older as per Vaidika tradition. Of the 200-odd Upanishads that are available today, ten are considered the most authoritative or principal Upanishads. These are the Isha, Kena, Katha, Prashna,

Mundaka, Maandookya, Taittareeya, Aitreya, Chhandogya and Brihadaaranyaka Upanishads, as laid down succinctly in this mnemonic verse:

ईशकेनकठप्रश्न – मुण्डमाण्डूक्यतित्तिरि ।
ऐतरेयं च छान्दोग्यं बृहदारण्यकं तथा ॥

Upanishads form part of the Vaidika lore, which consists of four parts:

Sanhitaa – This is another name for the Vedas proper, the revealed portion.

Braahmana – These are oldest available commentaries on the Vedas. They seem to be describing Yajnas and very symbolic stories. They are not very well understood today. However, they still assist in decoding the Vedas.

Aaranyaka – These are also very ancient and typically go hand-in-hand with the Braahmanas. They further elaborate the Karmakaanda and Jnaanakaanda of the Vedas.

Upanishad – These are typically those parts of the Braahmana or Aaranyaka that is devoted to Adhyaatma-vidyaa – spiritual knowledge. Ishopanishad is even part of a Veda itself! They constitute mostly Jnaanakaanda and Upaasanaakaanda.

Each of the last three is associated with a particular Veda.

The word 'Upanishad' is made up of Upa (close) + Ni (properly, down) + Shad (to sit or obtain), thus implying knowledge that is to be obtained properly by sitting close to a teacher. In Indian tradition, the Guru is considered absolutely essential to obtain the highest spiritual knowledge. This is what the name, too, implies. Another name for the Upanishad is Rahasya, or mystery, since it contains knowledge beyond the senses. Mainly concentrating on the relationship of the Individual Soul with God, they have little Materialistic content.

Basic Philosophical Concepts

Understanding the following basic concepts of Indian spiritual thought, which are based on Vaidika precepts, is essential for beginners to grasp the Upanishad properly.

1) There are three eternal entities in this Universe:

   a) Inanimate matter, or **Prakrti**.

   b) Individual souls, **Jeevaatmaas**, that reside in each living being and are animate.

   c) The one Supreme Soul, **Paramaatmaa**, or God, who is animate and is the creator, controller and destroyer of the Universe. He is omnipresent, omniscient and metes out justice to the Jeevaatmaas based on their Karma (see below).

2) Prakrti has a base primordial form at the beginning of the Universe that transforms to yield the whole multiplicity of objects we see around us in the form of manifest matter. These transformations are transient on an astronomical scale, and return to their basic form upon complete destruction. See **Chart 1: The Order of Creation** for the various transformations of primordial matter.

3) The Universe comes into existence as **Srshti**. It expands and diversifies over the period of creation, or **Kalpa**. It ends in **Pralaya** when everything is reduced to its primordial form. This lasts as long as the Kalpa. The whole period of a Kalpa and Pralaya comprises a 'Day of Brahma'. The cycle repeats itself *ad infinitum*. Like a rotating wheel, it has no beginning or end. This may be termed a 'cyclical infinity'.

4) The Material body is the abode of the soul. When the body encompassing a soul dies, the soul continues to exist. It moves on to another body in an eternal cycle of birth, death and re-incarnation. God *never* occupies a body.

5) Living beings are born as different species, in a hierarchy starting from the plant world, moving on to viruses, bacteria, insects, fishes, amphibians, lower animals and mammals, to man, finally, at the top of the pyramid. Human birth is considered the pinnacle of Material existence, as humans have the most discerning intellect and the highest capacity for well-thought-out action vis-à-vis the largely instinctive behaviour of other creatures. Humans also have the maximum capacity for modifying and enjoying their environment. The soul, particularly in a human birth, is independent in performing its actions.

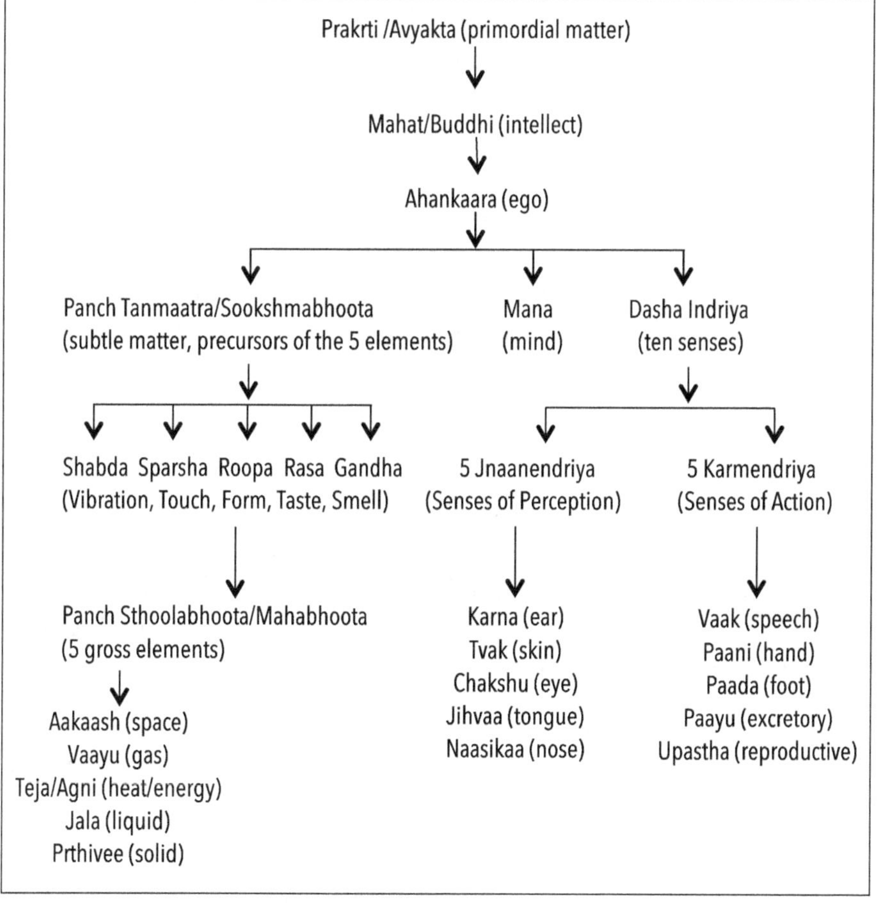

Chart 1: The Order of Creation

6) This structure is not unjust. It is based upon the deeds that a soul performs. Actions lead to equal reactions (as opposed to Newton's Third Law which states that action and reaction are equal and opposite!). Thus, a benevolent deed (Dharma/ Punya) results in happiness and a sinful deed (Adharma/ Paapa) leads to sorrow. Some deeds affect the soul's happiness in this birth; others come to fruition in future births. Happiness being a function of the species the soul is born into, Karmas also determine the species. Not only that, the length of the individual's lifespan is also a function of his/her Karma. This is the **Law of Action (Karma)**.

7) For the Law of Karma to be truly fair, the rules of the game should be known to the players. These rules are codified in the Vedas as Dharma, or righteousness, or ethics. The fact that the Vedas are not manmade can be surmised from the fact that they prescribe certain acts, which we would never associate as desirable, e.g., performing Yajnas for cleaning our environment, donating wealth to the needy, giving brains priority over brawn, salvation. Those who act as per their Dharma attain happiness in this birth and/or the next; those who do not are doomed to suffer.

8) While the Cycle of Life and Death continues endlessly, it is possible for a soul to exit the cycle by means of salvation, or **Moksha**. This is a non-obvious path that cannot be reasoned out by any available data. Therefore, it forms the subject matter of all the Upanishads in particular, and other spiritual texts in general. This path is detailed by the Vedas and corroborated by enlightened sages.

9) The Vedas and other philosophical texts based on them set out the order of the Creation of this Universe, which is the same in every epoch, since God's creation is perfect to begin with and does not require any 'evolution' to improve upon things!

10) The Vedas specify **four goals** for humans. These allow a

person to lead a fulfilling life. These include:

a) **Dharma:** Righteousness in all actions and the performance of duties towards ourselves, our families, our society, our nation, the world, the environment and all the creatures that live in it.

b) **Artha:** means wealth and includes all activities that result in the generation of wealth. Our jobs are a typical example. All economic activities are covered here.

c) **Kaama:** An individual works primarily for the fulfilment of desires. All these are covered by Kaama. All the needs, comforts and pleasures of life are part of Kaama.

d) **Moksha:** This is, of course, the highest goal – the release from the Cycle of Birth and Death.

While the first three goals are worldly in nature, the fourth is 'other-worldly'. Thus, while all adults will participate in Dharma, Artha and Kaama in some way or the other, very few will renounce everything and go on a quest for the third entity in this world – God.

11) The Vedas further detail how a normal life should be lived. They divide the average human life of 100 years (something we will find unbelievable today!) into four equal parts of 25 years each, called Aashramas, i.e., where effort is put. The activities during these parts are as follows:

a) **Brahmacharya-ashrama:** or student years. The time for gathering knowledge in schools, colleges and universities. Even today, most of us do not spend 25 years studying!

b) **Grhastha-ashrama:** or living as a householder. When one enters a job and/or matrimony. While one was dependent on others in the first phase, the whole society is dependent on the householder. They are the engines of the economy and create wealth and prosperity for the nation.

c) **Vaanprastha-ashrama:** At about the age of 50 years, one should give up worldly responsibilities and head for seclusion. In ancient days, people went to the forests, and maybe entered a sage's Aashrama (simple abode of spiritual seekers living together as a community) or lived separately in a hut. In today's times, it is alright to take up spiritual studies in the confines of one's home, coupled with simple living and interaction with like-minded people.

d) **Sanyaasa-ashrama:** or renunciation. When one has achieved a certain level of enlightenment and is ready to renounce worldly living altogether, one enters this Aashrama and spends the rest of his time in meditation and preaching. The Sanyaasi roams from town to town visiting householders, accepting food from them and giving them spiritual guidance, in turn. Ideally, the Sanyaasi does not stay in the householder's home, but rather away from habitation in a temple or a cave or some such natural abode.

Looked at another way, the first 25 years are spent learning Dharma. The next quarter century is spent applying Dharma to enjoy Artha and Kaama. In Vaanaprastha, one gives up Artha and Kaama and turns towards Moksha. Achieving success in that enterprise, he then becomes a Sanyaasee. There is no hard and fast rule about the number of years here, nor of following the guidelines strictly. Thus, one can jump from Brahmacharya to Sanyaasa, or one can continue in Grhasthaashrama till death. This structure just defines the ideal human life.

12) The Vedas have laid out five primary responsibilities of human beings towards knowledge and its enhancement, towards elders, other humans, other beings and the environment. These are called the Pancha Mahayajna (the five great works) and are particularly important for the householder (= Grhasthee). The five are as follows:

a) **Brahmayajna** – Learning and teaching particularly of the Vedas. Self-study should be continued throughout life.

b) **Devayajna** – Performing homas to cleanse the toxins from the environment and promote the health and well-being of all plants and animals.

c) **Pitryajna** – Serving the living elders and ensuring their happiness and well-being.

d) **Atithiyajna or Nryajna** – Taking care of guests, particularly the Sanyasees who come for alms and impart spiritual knowledge to the householder in return.

e) **Bali-vaishwa-deva-yajna** or **Bhootayajna** – setting aside some food for the lower forms of life, like ants, crows, etc., and even needy human beings, like lepers, the homeless, etc.

It is always so amazing to see this wholesomeness of Vaidika precepts: they preach the importance of all creation towards our well-being. They preach gratitude towards everyone and everything that shapes our lives. They preach sharing and taking care of all. From these teachings alone one can extrapolate that the divisive practices that are followed in the name of the Vedas are definitely not the true teaching of the Vedas. Of course, these teachings are far ahead of any other way of life being taught and/or practised in any other part of the ancient world, or even in today's world, for that matter.

13) The Vaidika ideology requires one to be extremely scientific. The quest for Moksha is seen as a quest for the ultimate truth. Therefore, it is incumbent on the seeker to learn the tools for discriminating between truth and falsehood. This is encapsulated in four **Pramaanas** by Sage Gautama in Nyaayadarshana. These are as follows:

a) **Pratyaksha** – This is direct witnessing by the senses. If the information generated by any of the senses is not occluded or dubious in any way, then it should be regarded as the truth.

The extra-sensory perception of Yogees is acceptable under this category.

b) **Anumaana** – Starting with known premises, to arrive at a logical conclusion. Typically, the starting point for the reasoning process will be something that is witnessed directly, i.e., Pratyaksha.

c) **Upamaana** – To elucidate by means of a well-known example or analogy. Thus, one may say, 'All stars are like the Sun.' Since the Sun is understood well, we can comprehend the other stars, too, that are beyond the range of our perception.

d) **Shabda** – A fact verified by Pratyaksha and/or Anumaana by an expert can now be taught to another, without the latter having to necessarily undergo either of the two processes himself. This may seem a little doubtful to some. However, we come to know most things in life like this. For example, Neil Armstrong was the first man to step on the moon is a fact that neither you, nor I have seen with our own eyes. If we do not want to believe the 'reliable sources' that tell us this, we will forever remain ignorant of the fact that man has reached the moon.

Explanatory Note on Vaidika Words

Vaidika words are vast in their meaning. They are derived from a root and a combination of prefixes and suffixes. Each of these components has one or more meanings, and influences the meaning of the final word. The meaning so derived is called Yaugika meaning, and each word can have many Yaugika meanings. Which meaning is applicable at a particular location is determined based on the context, and is left to the experts in the field to decide – the sages. This is how Vaidika words differ from common words, called Laukika Shabdas, which are restricted to a single meaning, or at the most two or three. For example, in English, the Laukika word 'well', could mean a repository of water, or health, or goodness, or just an interjection. In this case, too, the context determines the appropriate meaning of the word to be chosen. In the case of Vaidika words, the number of meanings is so vast that it requires a different kind of intelligence to figure out which meaning is applicable. To make matters more complex, more than one meaning can be applicable simultaneously or separately in a single mantra, giving it different hues like the colours in the rainbow!

Take the Vaidika word 'Brahma', which is used very often in the Upanishads. It has several meanings depending on the context. Typically, it means the Supreme, i.e., God, but it could have many other meanings as well. Arising from the root 'Brh' meaning 'to be large' or 'to expand or 'to make a sound', the word can typically have the following meanings:

- Huge

- The Supreme because He is huge – larger than the Universe, in fact!

- The Universe, also called Brahmaanda, because it is huge

- The Vedas because they transmit the knowledge of large things – the Supreme, the Universe and life in general; or because they are a large repository of knowledge

- The Braahmana, i.e., the knower of the Vedas and/or the Supreme

- The Jeevaatmaa because it is much greater than inanimate Matter.

This multiplicity of meanings is found in the verses of the Upanishads, too, particularly where the verses are borrowed from the Vedas. I have tried to cover all these alternative meanings in my commentary.

In the Vedas, God occurs in all three genders – masculine, feminine and neuter. Sometimes multiple genders are found in the same verse. I have tried to translate the Sanskrit verse literally with the gender as given. This makes for some awkward reading in English at times, but I think the readers will appreciate the closeness of the translation to the original. Also, I have tried to address this awkwardness in the ensuing explanation.

EXPLANATORY NOTES ON THIS COMMENTARY

1. The first paragraph of the commentary following a verse is as close to a literal translation of the verse as possible and is in italics. Brackets are generally used to indicate the 'unsaid' in the verse, the meaning of a word/phrase or, sometimes, the Sanskrit word being referred to. Sometimes, in the interest of readability, the brackets have been done away with.

2. The following paragraph(s) contains a detailed explanation of the verse to fully understand its purport.

3. The word 'Soul' always refers to the individual soul, or Jeevaatmaa, and very rarely to Paramaatmaa, in which case it is mentioned clearly as such.

4. Sanskrit words have been capitalised. Instead of diacritical marks to denote their correct pronunciation, devices such as 'aa' to represent ā, 'ee' for ī, etc., have been used to simplify the reading experience.

5. Some English words have also been capitalised in order to emphasise their unique usage. For example, 'Matter' is used to denote 'the physical substance, the thing that objects are made up of', and the capital M distinguishes it from its other meanings, viz., subject or problem.

6. In general, words in the male gender include the female gender and vice versa.

The Word of God
Ishopanishad

CONTENTS

Introduction to Ishopanishad 25

Ishopanishad: The Realm of the Lord 27

Introduction to Ishopanishad

Isha occupies pride of place at the head of the Upanishads. This is because it is actually part of a Veda, the Shukla Yajurveda[1], to be precise. Ishopanishad is the fortieth and last chapter of this Veda. No other Upanishad is a part of the Vedas; they are usually sections of a Braahmana or an Aaranyaka, which are the oldest commentaries on the Vedas available today. For this reason, this Upanishad is considered the first among the Upanishads. 'Ishaa' being the first word of the first verse, it is called Isha Upanishad, or Ishopanishad. The first two words being 'Ishaa vaasya', it is also called Ishaa-vaasya Upanishad, or Ishaavaasyopanishad. Being at the end of one of the Vedas, it is also called Vedaanta.

Ishopanishad lives up to the ideal of an Upanishad: It largely discusses salvation (Moksha), but it also describes the proper way of life for a normal worldly person. It gives an idea of all the three entities of the Universe,[2] especially dwelling on God – the unseen entity.

Tradition holds that the author of this work, as of all the Vedas, is the Supreme Itself. The Vedas are considered Apaurusheya, or not created by man. The Lord seeded them as-is in the minds of sages at the beginning of human creation. Thus, Rgveda was revealed to

---

1 This is considered the original Veda, while the other – Krshna Yajurveda – is a recension of it.
2 See Introduction, point 1.

Sage Agni, Yajurveda to Sage Vaayu, Saamaveda to Sage Aaditya and Atharvaveda to Sage Angiraa. They transmitted all the four Vedas to Brahmaa. From Brahmaa, a continuous line of sages and preachers kept the knowledge alive down the millennia till it reached us today, almost intact.

While the Ishopanishad is essentially the last chapter of the Shukla Yajurveda, the order of the verses in the Upanishad that is prevalent today is slightly different from that in the Veda, and some of the verses have been modified. This was done by ancient masters in the days of yore to make the subject matter easier for their students. This commentary is unique in that it covers both the Vaidika and the Upanishadic versions. The Vaidika chapter has 17 verses, while the Upanishad has 18 verses.

These verses typically follow the Anushtup or Trishtup meters, while a few verses are found in Jagatee and Ushnika meters also. Anushtup and Trishtup are very popular metres in Sanskrit works.[3]

____

3 *For the curious, here is some more information: The main subject (Devataa) of the Vaidika verses in this Upanishad is Aatmaa, except for verse 4, where the Devataa is Brahma. Thus, the verses refer to the individual Soul in most cases, and to God in the fourth one. The subordinate subject (Rshi) of all the verses is Deerghaatmaa, which seems to refer to the elongation of life by the knowledge given in the verses – essentially that of Dharma. Thus, the purport of the verses, if translated into action, will lead to longevity.*

Ishopanishad: The Realm of the Lord

The famous first verse of the Upanishad describes the proper way to live life. The message it gives is so profound that it is rarely found in any other religion of the world. Each word must be dwelt upon and deliberated over, for there is a wealth of meaning here:

ईशा वास्यमिदं सर्वं यत्किञ्च जगत्यां जगत् ।

तेन त्यक्तेन भुञ्जीथा मा गृधः कस्य स्विद्धनम् ॥ १॥

Whatever moves/changes in this world is permeated by Isha (the Lord of everything). For this reason, enjoy it with renunciation. Don't be greedy, (for) whose wealth is it anyway?!

Everything in this world is changing all the time. Change is inevitable in every atom, every molecule in this whole Universe. God is the ultimate controller of these changes and, in this way, He is the Lord of everything in the Universe. Know this, and accept all your belongings, including your body, as a temporary gift from Him, for nothing is really yours. It is as if He has rented it out to you for the duration of your life. You can enjoy things, just as you enjoy a rented house. But, in the final analysis, it is all His anyway. So, desist from becoming excessively possessive, or greedy, about anything. If you see Him as pervading each and every object, the feeling of non-covetousness will automatically arise in you.

The word 'Jagat' stands for the world in common parlance. However, in the verse, that is called 'Jagatee', inherent in the word 'Jagatyaam'. The word 'Jagat', on the other hand, implies movement or change, as it is derived from the verb root 'Gaml' meaning movement (also 'knowing' and 'attaining' – meanings that are not applicable here).

The word, 'Kasya' has two potential meanings: 'whose' or 'Ka's'. 'Ka' is another name for God, meaning 'the One who is always happy' and 'the One who gives happiness'. With these two meanings, we get a pun in the last part of the verse. The simple meaning is the rhetorical question "For whose wealth is it anyway?" At the same time, a deeper meaning unfolds: "In fact, all wealth is really Ka's." And that is why wealth gives pleasure, too!

The next verse continues the thought –

कुर्वन्नेवेह कर्माणि जिजीविषेच्छतं समाः ।
एवं त्वयि नान्येथोऽस्ति न कर्म लिप्यते नरे ॥ २ ॥

Desire to live in this world for (at least) a hundred years while remaining active. In this way, and in this way alone, will your deeds not stick to you who are a human being.

The 'right way to live' is given here in conjunction with the previous verse, i.e., consume the pleasures of this world without being attached to them and desire to live long. Usually, enjoyment of Material pleasures generates a craving for them. However, the right way is to enjoy what comes your way, by your rightful effort; but in case some effort does not yield the desired result, do not fret. This message is famously encapsulated in the following verse of Bhagawad-geeta:

कर्मण्येवाधिकारस्ते मा फलेषु कदाचन ।
मा कर्मफलहेतुर्भूर्मा ते सङ्गोऽस्त्वकर्मणि ॥ भगवद्गीता २।४७ ॥

You only have the right to perform an action, but never to its consequence (that is in the hands of God). Do not perform actions desiring its result; nor should you desist completely from action. Of course, this is a difficult recipe – for how do we perform deeds without desiring the goal? The answer is that the end-result is what determines the course of our efforts, but having performed the deed, we should give it up as an offering to God. This is called 'Eeshwara-pranidhaana', or surrender to God.

Ideally, when we are not attached to worldly things, we automatically perform only the deeds worth doing – our duties, our Dharma. There being no desire involved, the consequence of the action also does not 'stick'. 'Sticking' implies bearing fruit, as in happiness and sorrow, at a later point.

Also, when we desire to live long, we typically lead a very controlled, moderate life, giving up excesses like drinking and smoking. We make all efforts to stay mentally and physically fit. The Vedas endorse this. Note here that a century is considered an average lifespan for a human. Today, this can only be considered an extremely difficult goal to achieve! Learning from the lives of those who have managed to live long can help us live a healthy life, too. The mantra exhorts us to always wish and pray for a 100-year lifespan spent doing good deeds, and so, in the service of God. Many other Vaidika prayers contain this message with refrains like "Jeevema Sharadah Shatam" – May we live a hundred autumns.

The word 'Nara' means 'the one who leads'. Man is supposed to take initiative in improving his and others' lives, a trait not very well developed in any of the other animals. Also, it signifies that Man takes his own decisions. That is why the fruit of the action also applies to him. Animals, typically, use only instinct in their actions. These do not bear fruit. Theirs is like a jail term where the Soul is bound to lead a life controlled by others. The consequences of an animal's actions cannot then be blamed on it.

Continuing the theme of how to live one's life, the Upanishad now warns of the negative side of not leading a righteous life –

असुर्य्या नाम ते लोका अन्धेन तमसावृताः ।
ताँस्ते प्रेत्यापि गच्छन्ति[1] ये के चात्महनो जनाः ॥ ३ ॥

There are locations/situations that are called 'breath-serving' and are covered with blinding darkness. Those who go against their Soul, go to such places upon their death or even during this life.

'Asu' means breath and 'Yaa' means to go to. The Lokas, or species, in which the creature serves only its breath, i.e., its bodily cravings, are then called 'Asuryaa'. We can see this in all animals other than humans. Of course, even among humans, there are only a handful who look for spiritual enlightenment!

Darkness can be interpreted both literally and figuratively. Literally, there are many species that do not 'see' light, e.g., bacteria, viruses, earthworms, creatures found deep in the oceans, plants and trees. Their knowledge and enjoyment of this world is much more restricted than the creatures that possess eyes. Figuratively, darkness is equated with ignorance. While all plant and animal species are generally low on intelligence and, therefore, knowledge, even as a human one can be born into an ignorant, i.e., dark, existence. More importantly, one can induce ignorance in this birth itself due to one's deeds. For example, people who get addicted to drugs can fall into 'darkness' – getting disconnected from reality and retreating from activities that profit oneself and/or society.

'Going against one's Soul' is to act against one's conscience, to indulge in evil deeds. The word 'Aatmahana' literally means 'one who kills his/her own Soul'. Acts of cruelty, indulging in activities that destroy the mind and/or the body, etc., are all equivalent to 'killing oneself', literally and figuratively. God has given this life to follow the path of righteousness. Even though we may not be learned in Dharma (Ethics), God has a placed 'a still small voice' within us that constantly warns us when we are about to perform a wrong deed. The more we ignore that 'Voice of God', the worse

---

1 In the Upanishad, 'प्रेत्यापि गच्छन्ति' reads as 'प्रेत्याभिगच्छन्ति'. The meaning of both is the same.

the consequences.

The Upanishad now takes up the arduous task of describing the Supreme with all His contradictions –

अनेजदेकं मनसो जवीयो नैनद्देवा आप्नुवन् पूर्वमर्षत् ।
तद्धावतोऽन्यानत्येति तिष्ठत् तस्मिन्नपो मातरिश्वा दधाति ॥ ४ ॥

The One (God) does not move at all, and yet is faster than the mind. The senses cannot reach It because It is already there. It overtakes the senses that are running (after sense-objects), while remaining still. The Soul performs actions while residing within It.

This is a loaded verse, saying many things all at once, and revealing the contradictory nature of God, which is something like Alice's Wonderland, where the White Queen runs, yet does not move an inch!

Firstly, it points out the omnipresence of God. There is no place in this Universe that one can reach, even with the mind – the fastest thing in the Universe – where God does not exist already.

That the mind is the fastest thing in the Universe is implicit in the verse. This speed is not in terms of reaching a point in space, but rather in moving from subject to subject, so much so that we often think we are doing two things at a time, while actually our mind is flicking from one task to the other at lightning speed!

The verse also tells us that we cannot see God by means of the senses. The senses are constantly running after their sense-objects. If we keep following them, we will not reach anywhere near God. To reach It, we have to 'leave them behind' in deep meditation. This implies that repeating a stotra 1008 times, or paying obeisance to a stone statue, or taking a dip in the Ganga, may give us some side-benefits like increasing memory, mental focus, cleanliness, etc., but definitely not a vision of God.

The last quarter of the verse has words that have Yaugika

meanings (based on the root words). They are often misinterpreted by using the Laukika (common) meanings instead.[2] Thus, the usual meaning of 'Apa' is water. However, here it stands for deeds, actions. 'Maatarishwaa' usually denotes God, sometimes in a particular form. In the Vedas, however, the word is pregnant with much more meaning. Maatari means 'in space', while Shwaa means the act of breathing. Together the words imply a living being that breathes in the space provided by the Universe. In the original state of the Soul that is non-Material and occupies no space, it is incapable of acting upon this world. It is only the body that allows it to perform actions, impelled by its desire for worldly experiences. All these actions are observed by the Almighty, because they are occurring within Him!

Continuing to describe the seemingly contradictory nature of God, the next verse says –

तदेजति तन्नैजति तद्दूरे तद्वन्तिके ।
तदन्तरस्य सर्वस्य तदु सर्वस्यास्य बाह्यतः ॥ ५ ॥

It moves, (and yet) It does not move. It is far, (and yet) It is close. It is inside everything, (and yet) It is outside everything in this world.

It is an axiom in Indian philosophy that that which is Sarvavyaapaka (omnipresent) cannot move, because where does it move to?! Therefore, God does not move. However, It may seem to move through Creation itself, because in our limited understanding, objects can be made only by action, i.e., movement. However, this represents our inadequacy to understand the nature of God and Its actions. Therefore, for the ignorant, God appears to move, while in reality It does not move at all.

Similarly, It is very far from the ignorant or wicked person, but the learned seer or the righteous person experiences Its presence close by – within their Souls, in fact.

---

2 *See Introduction, Explanatory Note on Vaidika Words.*

It pervades both inside and outside all creatures and inanimate objects, i.e., everything in this Universe. Among the Trinity of Eternals, God is the subtlest, the Soul next and Matter the least subtle. Now, only the subtler can pervade the grosser. This may be understood as follows: If we put stones, sand and then water in a jar, the sand will fill the interstices between the stones and the water that between the sand particles, and not the other way around. Similarly, the Soul resides inside the Matter composing the body and God exists inside and outside of everything – Matter and Souls.

The next two verses should be read together. They elaborate the state of those who start perceiving the above-mentioned omniscience of God –

यस्तु सर्वाणि भूतान्यात्मन्नेवानुपश्यति[3] ।
सर्वभूतेषु चात्मानं ततो न विचिकत्सति[4] ॥ ६ ॥

The one who, having performed the practices of Yoga, starts seeing all created objects – living or non-living – inside Paramaatma, and also Paramaatma inside all of them, he then sheds all his doubts.

It is possible to understand intellectually that God permeates everything, thus being both inside and outside objects and Souls. But this does not remove doubts about the nature of Creation, the purpose of one's life – even the nature of God, in fact. Perceiving something directly is the only way to obtain all one's answers. It is only when one performs Yoga as taught by Patanjali in his immortal text, *Yogadarshanam*, and achieves Samaadhi, that all of Creation becomes clear – its nature, its purpose, one's place in it, etc.; above all, one gets a glimpse of the omnipresent Supreme. This last removes even the most stubborn doubts that may persist in the seeker.

---

3 *In the Upanishad, '*भूतान्यात्मन्नेवानुपश्यति*' is replaced by '*भूतान्यात्मन्येवानुपश्यति*'. The meaning, however, remains unaltered.*

4 *In the Upanishad, '*विचिकत्सति*' is replaced by '*विजुगुप्सते*'. The meaning of the last part then becomes: Then, he does not detest anybody.*

The Yoga prescribed by Patanjali is a little different from the one that we follow today, which is almost entirely restricted to body postures (Aasana) and breath-control (Praanaayaama), with some preliminary focusing of the mind (called meditation, but technically it is Pratyaahaara). Patanjali's text, on the other hand, focuses almost entirely on the control of the mind to achieve Samaadhi, or deep meditation.

The fact that practising Yoga is essential to this realisation is not obviously present in the verse and could be missed by the person not well versed in the Vedas. It is encapsulated in the prefix 'Anu' in the verb 'Anupashyati'. 'Anu' typically means 'following something', e.g., "Sita Ramam Anugacchati" means "Sita follows Rama". In the same way, here 'Anupashyati' implies that some practice has been performed earlier following which this vision is achieved; that is the practice of Yoga.

यस्मिन्त्सर्वाणि भूतान्यात्मैवाभूद्विजानतः ।
तत्र को मोहः कः शोक एकत्वमनुपश्यतः ॥ ७ ॥

Knowing all beings to be located inside God (as described above), just as one's own self, what attachment/delusion and what sorrow can there be? (That is, there is no sorrow or attachment for the person seeing this unity of all beings within that great One).

While each Soul is different in its nature, yet they are all similar as they all reside within God and are all trying to achieve their goals in their own way. When we perceive everyone as equal to us, we leave our evil, selfish, greedy nature, and treat each one as we would like to be treated. However, at the same time, we do see each Soul as independent, and not really related to us in any way. This removes our attachment/hatred for them. Even desires for Material objects are lost as the true nature of the Soul is realised. This detachment from the animate and the inanimate, in turn, ensures that we do not need to grieve for anything.

The pre-eminence of God in the state of enlightenment described in the above two verses makes our ultimate goal clear – the achievement of closeness with Him. So, the next verse describes in detail the nature of the One we are searching for –

स पर्यगाच्छुक्रमकायमव्रणमस्नाविरं शुद्धमपापविद्धम् ।
कविर्मनीषी परिभूः स्वयम्भूर्याथातथ्यतोऽर्थान् व्यदधाच्छाश्वतीभ्यः समाभ्यः ॥ ८॥

He is (Pari-agaat) omnipresent, (Shukra) quick, (Akaaya) without a body, (Avrana) does not have a wound or a gap in Its being and cannot be cut or torn to create such a gap (i.e., there is no point in space that does not have Him), (Asnaavira) does not have sinews (i.e., a gross body with organs, etc.), (Shuddha) pure (i.e., devoid of ignorance/delusion created by the body), (Apaapaviddha) unadulterated by sin (i.e., does not commit a sin, does not make anybody commit a sin and does not promote sin in any way whatsoever). (Kavi) His knowledge goes beyond all (i.e., He is omniscient). (Maneeshee) He knows the minds of all beings. (Paribhoo) He subjugates the sinners (i.e., they cannot get away from His justice). (Swayambhoo) He comes into being on His own (without anyone's support). He provides sense-objects to the eternal beings (embodied Souls) as they merit (i.e., according to the deeds they have performed); alternatively, for the eternal beings (particularly, human beings), he provides knowledge of the Universe (in the Vedas).

There are many words here whose meanings differ from the commonly accepted meanings today, e.g., Shukra, Kavi, Maneeshee. This is due to the meanings being Yaugika rather than Laukika.[5]

God is Shukra, or quick, because there is no time-gap between His thought and His act, the act happens immediately.

He has no body and no organs like our body (Asnaavira). We have become used to the concept of Avataaras today, where God walks the earth in a human or animal body, but this concept is a later addition

---

5 See Introduction, Explanatory Note on Vaidika Words.

started by the Puraanas, which are essentially mythology with little basis in truth. To a thinking mind, it should be immediately obvious that if God has to be omnipresent and omniscient, He cannot possibly be restricted in Space and Time. Also, bodies always lead to disease, pain, wounds (Vrana), etc. Bodies are made up of Matter – the five elements that make up this Universe. To acquire such a body, one has to be born and then shed it through death. God is unencumbered by any such frailty, by birth or by death.[6]

Shuddha is usually understood as bodily cleanliness, and sometimes also as mental cleanliness. In addition to these meanings, there is one more meaning – ignorance or Klesha, and the delusion caused by it are considered the main causes of impurity impacting a Soul. This ignorance lies at the root of all other impurities of the mind and body. God is devoid of all of these.

This ignorance further leads to sin. Since God is not bound by ignorance, He is also incapable of sins. A question sometimes arises that if God is omnipotent and can do everything He wishes then can He commit sin, too? The verse gives the answer to this question – a resounding No! While God creates, maintains and destroys the Universe, He will never do anything unjust and reprehensible. That would be tantamount to going against His essential nature.

The fact that this God subjugates everything and everyone else implies that there are no multiple gods, each with a subset of powers, overpowering each other every now and then. Nor is there a Satan that defies God every now and then. God is supreme, and nobody is equal to Him, let alone more than Him. At the beginning of Creation, He awakens, so to speak, and sets things in motion, requiring nobody's help to thus 'come into existence'.[7] For this reason, He is Swayambhoo.

---

6 *The Avataaras mentioned in the various stories handed down to us have sexual desires, are hurt by arrows, take birth only in the landmass of India, etc. One should consider whether this can really define a being who is supposed to be above all other beings and metes out happiness and sorrow based on their actions. The Avataara concept is not endorsed by the Vedas.*
7 *Does existence have any meaning if it does not perform any action? Philosophically, none. That is why God is said to 'come into being' at the beginning of Creation, from the 'slumber' of Dissolution (Pralaya), even though He is eternal and exists all along.*

Vedas are the fountainhead of all knowledge. Humans would not proceed too far without the jumpstart provided by them.[8]

Another question that arises is: If God is kind and loving, how is He so ruthless in punishing the erring Soul? Isn't that a sin, too? The answer is that just as justice is served only when the guilty are punished in Man's world, so also it is in God's world. God cannot forgive the guilty just because they plead to Him. He has to ensure that the good are protected and the sinful are punished. However, when we are very remorseful for our deeds, He does give us strength to bear our troubles.

All these qualities are in contrast to the properties of the Jeevaatmaa. The Jeeva is limited in Space (though not in Time). There is a time lag between its thought and action. It acquires a Material body at birth, complete with all the necessary organs. This body can be inflicted with wounds or afflicted with disease. Having been born, it is bound to die. The body creates much ignorance of the true nature of the world, the Soul and God. It creates desires that make the Soul commit sins. Thus, the union of the Soul with the body is fraught with sorrow. However, without the body, the Soul is not *capable* of knowing everything. It has a Material mind that it uses for its purpose, but cannot directly gauge the mind of others. It is not able to always conquer evil. It is not in control of the fruits of its own actions, let alone those of others! Thus, the verse delineates the Soul from the Supreme.

The next three verses form a set and should be read together. They describe the importance of knowledge in the attainment of Moksha, or salvation.

---

8 *This may seem a hyberbole at the outset. To understand it, think of how far some of the ancient civilisations went that had no Vedas to help them, e.g., the aborigines of many countries, and then compare them with those who did, e.g., the Indians who then transmitted it to the Chinese, Greeks, Egyptians, Arabs, most of the Asian and European countries and many more around the world, directly or indirectly. Of the myriads of things transmitted, only one will suffice to illustrate the power of the Vedas: The decimal system that is now acknowledged to be a necessary condition for higher Mathematics has its origins in the Vedas.*

अन्धन्तमः प्र विशन्ति येऽसम्भूतिमुपासते ।
ततो भूय इव ते तमो य उ सम्भूत्याँ रताः ॥ ९॥

Those who worship primordial unmanifest Matter (Prakrti, called Asambhooti here) enter blinding darkness; but those who are engrossed in manifest Matter (Sambhooti – which makes up the Universe around us) enter a darkness that is even greater.

Those who think that primordial Matter is all that everything breaks down into have studied the nature of the Universe in great detail and come to this conclusion. Not finding any sign of the Soul or God, they do not accept their existence. They never discover the spiritual realm. Because of this, they remain limited in their understanding of this world. Then, there are those who are engaged in consuming this manifest world and do not even care for the deeper mysteries of Matter. They are stuck in even greater ignorance, for they do not even know the nature of Matter!

Any knowledge of reality is considered a step towards enlightenment. Only indulging in Bhoga (consumption), with no regard to Jnaana (Knowledge) is considered the basest human existence.

अन्यदेवाहुः सम्भवादन्यदाहुरसम्भवात् ।
इति शुश्रुम धीराणां ये नस्तद्विचचक्षिरे ॥ १०॥

They say that the relevance of manifest Matter (towards the achievement of personal goals) is different, and that of unmanifest (primordial) Matter is different.[9] This is what we hear from the spiritual masters who have explained these matters to us in detail.

Neither manifest Matter, nor unmanifest Matter, is actually meaningless. It is just that they are not the be-all and end-all in this world, and must be seen for what they are. Also, they should

---

9 See Introduction, point 2.

be used judiciously, as described in the next verse.

The spiritual world is not available for empirical validation; it has to be understood from the masters who have seen the ultimate truth in their meditations. For this reason, it is imperative for the spiritual seeker, looking for answers to her nagging doubts, to seek out the right teacher(s).

सम्भूतिं च विनाशं च यस्तद्वेदोभयं सह ।
विनाशेन मृत्युं तीर्वा सम्भूत्यामृतमश्नुते ॥ ११ ॥

The one who knows both the manifest and unmanifest (primordial) Matter together goes beyond death by the help of primordial Matter, and by means of the manifest Matter attains salvation.

Here, the unmanifest Matter is called 'Vinaasha', literally meaning destruction, as that is the Matter that everything is reduced to at the end of the Universe. If we understand the properties of this Matter properly, we will understand that it cannot generate consciousness.[10] This, in turn, will prove to us irrefutably that the Soul *does* exist. Knowing ourselves to be different from Matter, we can then utilize our personal piece of Matter – our body – to transcend it and learn about the other entities involved, i.e., our Soul and God, in deep meditation (Samaadhi). Thus, both types of Matter are useful to us, and should be utilised in our quest for the ultimate truth.

The next three verses form a set similar to the above three. The first of these starts from where the previous set left off –

अन्धन्तमः प्र विशन्ति येऽविद्यामुपासते ।
ततो भूय इव ते तमो य उ विद्यायाँ रताः ॥ १२ ॥

---

10 Scientists do not usually accept the existence of the Soul. They see consciousness as an emergent property that is created by a special combination of matter. They have been trying to create life for a very long time. What they do not realize is that God has kept the creation of life – the uniting of a Soul with matter – as His own prerogative!

Those who are engrossed in the world and unable to discriminate between the body and the Soul, enter great ignorance. However, the ignorance of those is much greater who are limited to bookish knowledge.

The only difference between the previous set of three verses and this one is that the words Sambhooti and Asambhooti are replaced by Vidyaa and Avidyaa, respectively. So first, let us understand the latter two words. Avidyaa stands for mistaking the transient for the eternal, the impure for the pure, sorrow for joy, the inanimate for the animate, and vice versa, as per Maharshi Patanjali in *Yogadarshanam.*[11] For example, if one thinks that this body or this life is eternal, or if they believe that the impure body has been purified by ablutions or a bath, or if they believe that mundane experiences are blissful, or that the Matter making up the body is animate, then they are suffering from a delusion. In practical terms, Avidyaa translates into the Soul identifying with its body to such an extent that it spends its entire life catering to the cravings of the body and the mind.

Vidyaa, on the other hand, refers to a lack of the ignorance described above, and understanding reality the way it really is, primarily referring to the ability to discern between the Soul and the body. However, in this particular verse, 'people having Vidyaa' refers to those people who know this distinction only intellectually. Knowing only the literal meanings of the spiritual texts, they believe that they know it all. Without *experiencing* this Vidyaa, many things remain unknown and doubts continue to persist.

While the latter category of people should be more knowledgeable than those who are not even acquainted with spiritual truths, the verse declares them to suffer a worse fate when they do not apply their knowledge in real life. This is because the punishment for those who are aware of the truth, but still do not act according to it, is greater than those who are ignorant and act as they deem fit!

---

11 अनित्याशुचिदुःखानात्मसु नित्यशुचिसुखात्मख्यातिरविद्या (*Yogadarshanam, Chapter 2, verse 5)*

अन्यदेवाहुर्विद्याया अन्यदाहुरविद्यायाः ।
इति शुश्रुम धीराणां ये नस्तद्विचचक्षिरे ॥ १३ ॥

We hear from spiritual masters that true knowledge and wrong understanding – each has a role to play (in the attainment of their goals).

Neither true knowledge, nor wrong understanding are meaningless, and human beings should make use of both, as described in the next verse.

विद्यां चाविद्यां च यस्तद्वेदोभयँ सह ।
अविद्यया मृत्युं तीर्वा विद्ययामृतमश्नुते ॥ १४ ॥

The one, who knows both knowledge and its opposite, transcends death through ignorance, and attains Moksha through knowledge.

We saw earlier that Avidyaa refers primarily to the ignorance related to the body where we consider the body to be ourselves. This same body should be used to perform Dharma. Performance of Dharma tends to remove some fear of death from us (though we can be completely free of the fear of death only after enlightenment). This is 'transcending death'. Also, using the body, we do meditation (Upaasanaa), which leads us to the knowledge of the distinction between the body and the Soul, or enlightenment. It also gives us a glimpse of God. In this way, the delusion of oneness with the body is used by the wise to overcome that very same delusion!

This enlightenment of the true nature of the Soul leads to Amrta, or salvation. 'Amrta' means 'not dead'. In Moksha, there is no death because there is no birth – no union with Matter. Again we see that this meaning is Yaugika, different from the Laukika meaning of 'nectar that gives immortal life'. Absence of life is the true implication here.

The following verse in particular should be repeated at the time of death. In fact, by tradition, the following three verses are repeated at that time by the priest.

वायुरनिलममृतमथेदं भस्मान्तँ शरीरम् ।
ओ३म् क्रतो स्मर क्लिबे स्मर कृतँ स्मर ॥ १५॥

Air, subtle air and its primordial indestructible cause (i.e., the primordial Matter that transforms into air) – all these make up the body that ultimately ends in ashes. O Doer of deeds! Remember God for strength (in this time of weakness) and go over all the good and bad deeds that you have done in life.

First and foremost, the verse implies the eternity of the Soul, which is separate from the body, and is only escaping this abode at the time of death.

Next, 'air' implies all the five elements, or Panch Mahaabhootas, each of which has a subtle counterpart, called Sookshmabhoota or Tanmaatra. [12] The body itself is composed of three layers – the gross body which is visible to the eye and scientific instruments, the subtle body composed of subtle elements that can only be surmised, and a causal body that consists of primordial Matter. The last two are carried forward into the next life. These three bodies are being referred to here as Vaayu, Anila and Amrta.

The gross body should be consigned to flames at the end of life – this is the teaching of the Vedas, and is one of their non-trivial teachings. As you can see in other cultures of the world that have not been fully influenced by India, left to ourselves, we would not have the heart to burn our family member; burial seems so much more 'humane'! However, the Vedas tell us that the most environment-friendly thing to do is to let the body return to the environment once again – air to air, water to water, earth to earth – rather than make it the abode of worms and disease-carrying bacteria that pollute

---

12 See Introduction, point 2.

the soil, water and air, while taking centuries to decompose fully. [13]

Om is the name dearest to God. It is his personal name that nobody else shares (Om Puri and other Oms notwithstanding!). Om as a word occurs only twice among all the Vedas, and both those occurrences are found in this chapter. The verb root, Ava, from which it is derived, has the maximum number of meanings among all the roots – 21 in all – and all those meanings apply to God. Thus, this word provides the most expansive description of the Supreme. It is held in such high regard in the Indian tradition that Upanishad after Upanishad sings peons in its praise.[14]

It is always good to remember God at the time of death, but it is also recommended that we reflect on our life, and revise the lessons we have learnt, so that they are on the top of our mind in the next birth. Not only at the time of death, but chanting this verse during our lifetime will remind us of the ephemerality of this life and of the carrying forward of our Dharma and Adharma into our next life.[15] That will caution us in our actions. It will also create some detachment (Virakti) towards the world and our body. Therefore, repeat this verse every day – with the meaning ringing in your mind.

Having discussed the path to Moksha, the being makes a fervent appeal to God –

अग्ने नय सुपथा राये अस्मान्
विश्वानि देव वयुनानि विद्वान् ।
युयोध्यस्मज्जुहुराणमेनो
भूयिष्ठां ते नमउक्तिं विधेम ॥ १६ ॥

---

13 *Surprisingly, in Christianity, till today they say, 'Dust to dust, ashes to ashes.' However, the practice of reducing to ashes has been forgotten. It probably came from India and people picked up other practices again later. Somehow, only the words have survived.*
14 *It seems possible that the Christian Amen and the Islamic Ameen are derived from Om and that is why they are considered extremely holy words too, even though the significance of these words is not really clear there.*
15 *See Introduction, point 6.*

O Agni, the Enlightening One! Please take us on the righteous path towards Material, intellectual and spiritual wealth. O Deva, the Divine One! You know all about our nature and our deeds. So, please remove our crookedness and our wickedness from us. To this end, we respectfully bow before you and honour you repeatedly and immensely with eulogies.

There are several messages for the seeker here:

- The righteous path should be followed to attain wealth of any sort, be it Material, intellectual or spiritual. Acquisition of Material wealth is not looked down upon in Indian tradition; it is just that it is considered inferior to intellectual and spiritual gains.

- God is conversant with our innermost thoughts, as well as our external actions. For this reason, He is in the best position to guide us and take us on that righteous path.

- Crookedness, i.e., disparity in our thoughts, words and action, is one of the biggest sins. A spiritual seeker should strive to achieve unity in these three.

- While God does not revel in words of praise for Himself, those words endear Him to us, just like praising a loved one further endears the remembered person to the rememberer. Also, the qualities that we praise are those that we must try to acquire ourselves. That is, God's superlative qualities set a standard for us to follow. This, in turn, makes our goals clear and helps us to overcome our weaknesses.

Having so many positive prayers embedded in it, this verse should definitely be included in one's daily routine!

God now speaks to the Soul –

हिरण्यमयेन पात्रेण सत्यस्यापिहितं मुखम् ।

योऽसावादित्ये पुरुषः सोऽसावहम् । ओ३म् खं ब्रह्म ॥ १७॥[16]

---

16 *This mantra is also found in Rigveda 1|189|1, Yajurveda 5|36 and 17|43. This multiple occurrence reflects its importance.*

The face of truth is covered by a golden vessel. The person that is in Aaditya, that One is Me – Om, Kha, Brahma.

At first read, the verse makes little sense. That is because the words are extremely layered.

Here, truth, or Satya, is God Himself – the ultimate Truth, the ultimate Reality.

'Hiranyamaya Paatra' means a golden vessel. Here, it refers to the Universe. The Universe is called so because it encloses luminous bodies like the sun, stars, galaxies, etc., within itself. The verse is, thus, telling us that the fact of His presence is covered up by Nature, by the Universe. That is, God can never be discovered in Nature. That is why, till date, we have not been able to find God scientifically. Seeing the immutable laws that operate in Nature, and the intelligence inherent in Creation, the experienced among us can see the hand of God, but it is really very difficult to prove His existence empirically.

One of the meanings of Aaditya is Praana, or the life-breath. The verse subtly implies that the performance of Pranaayaama (control of the breath) leading to Upaasanaa (meditation) is the means to find God – to remove the cover of the golden vessel! However, Aaditya also means the Sun, as is commonly understood. Thus, this sentence also means: I can be found in the Sun. This hints at taking the brilliant Sun as a symbol for God, not as an idol or an animate being, but due to its effulgence. Even the vision of God is supposed to be full of radiance. So, this is an apt metaphor. Additionally, most people require a support in order to focus their mind and find it difficult to concentrate on a formless God. They then give some form to their God – a human figure, an animal figure, a plant, an inanimate object, etc. However, these are rather unrepresentative of God. God has Himself suggested the Sun as an appropriate representation. This does not mean that one should look directly at the Sun and blind oneself, but rather to focus on it in the mind.[17]

17 *A third meaning here is that liberated Souls reside in God on luminous stars. Reference to liberated Souls, devoid of any Material body, making luminous bodies their residence, so to speak, while they remain free to travel wherever they please in the Universe, is found at many places in the Vedas. However, this view is not accepted by all scholars.*

The last three words give the names and qualities that describe God best. Om implies, among other things, a protector. Kha usually refers to Space as it denotes pervasiveness. Brahma implies vastness. God being the ultimate Protector, the Pervader of space and larger than the Universe itself, all these adjectives are more than befitting for Him. These are the qualities that should be focussed on in Samaadhi in order to reach God.

The Upanishadic Version

The prevalent Upanishad differs from the Veda as follows:

- Verses 12-14 appear before Verses 9-11.

- Verses 15-16 have been put after Verse 17.

- The wordings of Verse 15 differ slightly.

- Verse 17 has been split into two and some additional words are added. Thus, the Vaidika chapter has 17 verses, while the Upanishad has 18 verses.

The verses in place of 15 and 17 are detailed below, with the verse numbers appropriate to the Upanishad, rather than the Veda.

The Vaidika verse 17 becomes a prayer by the devotee, rather than a direct message from God –

हिरण्यमयेन पात्रेण सत्यस्यापिहितं मुखम् ।
तत् त्वं पूषन्नपावृणु सत्यधर्माय दृष्टये ॥१५॥

The face of Truth (God) is covered by a golden vessel (the Universe). O Pooshan (Nurturer)! Please remove the cover to allow me, who has followed the path of truth and Dharma diligently, to see the true Dharma (God).

The word 'Satyadharmaaya' has two meanings here, one describing the devotee, the other, the object of the vision. The devotee says, "As per your command, I followed the path of truth and righteousness in my behaviour rigorously (Satya and Dharma), and you have nurtured me on that path. Now, please show me the ultimate truth, the ultimate Dharma (Satya Dharma) i.e., Yourself. You have hidden yourself by the cover of the Material world. You alone can gratify the devotee by removing this self-imposed golden cover."

Overcome with devotion, the seeker continues –

पूषन्नेकर्षे यम सूर्य प्राजा –
पत्य व्यूह रश्मीन् समूह ।
तेजो यत्ते रूपं कल्याणतमं तत्ते पश्यामि
योऽसावसौ पुरुषः सोऽहमस्मि ॥ १६॥

O Nurturer! O Solitary Seer! O Controller! O Effulgent One! O One having the qualities of the Lord of Beings! Arrange the beams and collect (your) brilliance, (so that) I may see that form of yours which is the most benevolent. The One that is (visible in the Sun is) that, that Person (God), He is (also) me.

This verse seems a bit confusing. Continuing from the previous verse, the devotee prays to the effulgent God that He may make His form available to the devotee's view. That is why he asks God to collect His over-powering brilliance into Himself as it is blinding him.[18] On seeing that form of God, his life will be sanctified. Just as God resides in the Sun and other inanimate objects, so also does God reside in the devotee and all other living creatures. Thus, the devotee sees God in each and every thing.

वायुरनिलममृतमथेदं भस्मान्तँ शरीरम् ।
ओ३म् क्रतो स्मर कृतँ स्मर क्रतो स्मर कृतँ स्मर ॥ १७॥

The vital breath (Praana), subtle air and its primordial indestructible cause (i.e., the primordial Matter that transforms into

---

18 This idea is similar to the Vishwaroopa of Krishna in the Geetaa that overwhelmed Arjuna.

air) – all these make up the body that ultimately ends in ashes. O Doer of Deeds! Remember God and your deeds (repeated twice for impact).[19]

Having taken the Soul from worldly duties to death to the attainment of Moksha, with a glimpse of the Supreme on the way, the Upanishad now draws to a close.

May Brahma enlighten us all!

---

19 See the detailed explanation at verse 15 earlier.

Grasping The Unknown

Kenopanishad

CONTENTS

Introduction to Kenopanishad 51

Section 1: The Hidden Motivator 52

Section 2: The Conundrum that is God 59

Section 3: The Parable of the Devas and Brahma 63

Section 4: The Parable Decoded 66

Introduction to Kenopanishad

Kena is a short and sweet Upanishad and is considered second in importance in the ranking of Upanishads, of which over 200 are available today. It asks fundamental questions about life and proceeds to illustrate them through a fable – in the typical style of the Upanishads.

Kena is the 9th chapter of the Talavakaara Braahmana of Saamaveda. For this reason, it is also called Talavakaar-opanishad. It is also called Jaimineeya and Braahmana Upanishad. However, it is most popularly known as Kena (Upanishad) based on the first word of the text. This Sanskrit word means 'by whom' and represents the central question being asked in the work – by whom is this beautiful Creation made? – an answer to which is not immediately available to the rational, thinking mind. The Upanishad has four chapters of which the first two are in verse and are devoted to describing Brahma and the one who knows Brahma; the last two chapters are in prose and further describe Brahma by means of a metaphorical tale. The meaning of the tale is not fully comprehended today. However, the primary essence is still available. It has only 8+5+12+9 = 34 verses. It has several verses that are extremely uplifting, are widely quoted and are worth memorising.

SECTION 1
The Hidden Motivator

The very first verse of Kenopanishad sets the tone for what the reader can expect from the rest of the Upanishad. It sets out the questions, as if asked by a student of the teacher, that will be answered later in the text. Indeed, the very name of the Upanishad is based on the first word of this verse – Kena – meaning 'by whom'. 'By whom' really summarises our search for the Divine, for is it not the phrase that precedes all our spiritual quests? – By whom has this Universe been created? By whom have I been given this life? By whom are all the events in my life ordained? These queries represent a philosophical search because the answer is hidden from us; only the teachings of the seers make us aware of who 'It' is. So does this Upanishad take up its quest –

केनेषितं पतति प्रेषितं मनः

केन प्राणः प्रथमः प्रैति युक्तः ।

केनेषितां वाचमिमां वदन्ति

चक्षुः श्रोत्रं क उ देवो युनक्ति ॥ १।१॥

By whom is the Mind motivated (to make the sense organ) to fall upon (perceive) the desired (sensory object)? By whom is the life-breath prompted to start its movements in the beginning (of life in a body)? By whom is speech prompted to speak? Which Divine Being conjoins the eye and the ear (to its sensory object – form and sound, respectively)?

The functions of the body and those of the senses, in particular, are often taken for granted by the common person. But for the philosopher there is a deep mystery in their functioning. This is also true for the biologist who studies the perception of stimuli by the senses, their transduction into electrical signals that are carried to specific areas of the brain where they are made sense of in terms of, say, colours, and then matched with previously collected data stored in the memory to draw conclusions about the environment. We can also appreciate how complex this process is by remembering that the 'very intelligent' Man has not yet been able to replicate even one of them to any substantial degree in any one of his own creations – machines.

The questions posed in the previous verse are answered now, as if by the teacher –

श्रोत्रस्य श्रोत्रं मनसो मनो
यद्वाचो ह वाचं स उ प्राणस्य प्राणः ।
चक्षुषश्चक्षुरतिमुच्य धीराः
प्रेत्यास्माल्लोकादमृता भवन्ति ॥ १।२॥

Decidedly, He (i.e., God) is the Ear of the ear, the Mind of the mind, the Speech of speech, the Breath of breath, and the Eye of the eye. (Knowing this truth), the steadfast ones (seers), becoming completely rid (of desires related to the senses), attain immortality on leaving this world.

God is the One who motivates all the senses, including the mind, into sensing this world, and starts the breath in a being. While it is true, that a being controls its senses to a large degree, the seer wants to take us one level deeper into that which is not obvious –

to reveal the ultimate Motivator. Without this Motivator, can even a finger be lifted?!

If God is the real Motivator, then where do we fit in? Why are we running to where our senses are taking us? When the Soul realises that this hankering after objects of the senses that makes up all our mundane desires is not really its true nature, it gives up those desires and turns inwards to connect with the Motivator. Finding Him, it achieves salvation.

The seer now explains the difficulty in understanding God through the senses or by known means of transmission of knowledge –

न तत्र चक्षुर्गच्छति न वाग्गच्छति नो मनो ।
न विद्मो न विजानीमो यथैतदनुशिष्यादन्यदेव तद्विदितादथो अविदितादधि ।
इति शुश्रुम पूर्वेषां ये नस्तद्व्याचचक्षिरे ॥ १।३॥

The eye cannot go there (reach Him), nor speech, nor the mind. We do not know Him, nor do we know how we can explain Him (to our disciples, because) It is quite different from that which is known, and beyond that which is unknown – this is what we have heard from the earlier seers who have preached to us.

Humans acquire learning by direct observation, by reasoning or by learning from others.[1] None of these methods opens a window to God because He is beyond the senses and the mind.

Speech is a human's primary tool for conveying knowledge gained by one to another. But, speech, too, falls far short in describing spiritual matters – in particular, God. No picture can describe Him, nor any idol represent Him. For this reason, in this verse, the seer describes his helplessness in leading his students towards the discovery of God. In fact, sometimes seers resort to the form of description called 'Neti, Neti' – It is not this, It is not this –

---

1 *Refer to the Introduction, point 13.*

giving a negative list of attributes of God rather than a positive one. The seer uses a similar device in the following verse –

यद्वाचानभ्युदितं येन वागभ्युद्यते ।
तदेव ब्रह्म त्वं विद्धि नेदं यदिदमुपासते ॥ १।४॥

That which is not described (brought to light) by speech, but by Whom speech describes, know That alone to be Brahma (the Great), not this which is worshipped (in this world).

The verse lays to rest all doubts that may linger regarding the answer to the questions asked in the first verse – God is the answer to all of them!

Some people believe that seers can describe the Lord in their sermons. The seer clarifies that no description can do justice to what He really is. Just as the eye does not see itself, God being the instrument of perception, He Himself is beyond perception. The Lord who is being worshipped in human, animal or even inanimate forms is not the one the seeker of truth is looking for.

The seer continues in the same vein –

यन्मनसा न मनुते येनाहुर्मनो मतम् ।
तदेव ब्रह्म त्वं विद्धि नेदं यदिदमुपासते ॥ १।५॥

That which cannot be thought of by the mind, but by Whom the mind thinks, know That alone to be Brahma (the Great), not this which is worshipped (in this world).

Some people believe that some thoughts, e.g., 'pure thoughts' of images of Nature, or the pursuit of the science of this Universe, can lead to salvation. That, too, falls short of the reality that is Him, clarifies the seer. This leads one to the conundrum that if my instrument of knowledge cannot perceive Him, how *do* I see Him?

The seer answers this important question in due course, but first he has to fully clarify what God is not –

यच्चक्षुषा न पश्यति येन चक्षूँषि पश्यन्ति ।
तदेव ब्रह्म त्वं विद्धि नेदं यदिदमुपासते ॥ १।६ ॥

That which cannot be seen by the eye, but by Whom the eyes see, know That alone to be Brahma (the Great), not this which is worshipped (in this world).

Some people believe that looking at some forms, e.g., the idols of gods, can lead to salvation. The seer confirms that that, too, is not going to happen. This is a sensitive issue in India as idol-worship has been in vogue at least since the time of Shankaraachaarya. The Puraanas were instrumental in starting this trend. Idols make the subject very accessible to all – the learned and the not-so-learned. Just as the diagram of a heart explains its functioning easily, while it really is quite far from reality, similarly an idol provides us with a form to love and adore, though there may be no basis for it. It is very difficult to think of and/or worship an abstract subject. But for the one seeking the ultimate truth, there is no other go, but to accept the formlessness of God.

The seer further emphasises, as if to drive the point home –

यच्छ्रोत्रेण न शृणोति येन श्रोत्रमिदँ श्रुतम् ।
तदेव ब्रह्म त्वं विद्धि नेदं यदिदमुपासते ॥ १।७ ॥

That which cannot be heard by the ears, but by Whom the ear hears, know That alone to be Brahma (the Great), not this which is worshipped (in this world).

Some people believe that some sounds, e.g., that of Om, or that of certain Raagas, can lead to salvation. The seer clarifies that these can never take you there. While certain sounds and their combinations can help us reach a higher meditative state, focusing on any of the sense-objects keeps us firmly fixed in this world and will not let us break its shackles.

The seer does not cover any further senses, as the eye and ear are representative of the remaining ones – of touch, taste and smell. The ear is covered separately as, after the eyes, it is the main sense for gaining knowledge of this world and beyond.

It is also worth noting that we have considered the primary means by which knowledge is gained – the speech of the teacher, the reasoning of the mind and perception by the senses.

However, there is perhaps one more way in which we may gain knowledge of the Supreme –

यत् प्राणेन न प्राणिति येन प्राणः प्रणीयते ।
तदेव ब्रह्म त्वं विद्धि नेदं यदिदमुपासते ॥ १।८ ॥

That which cannot be breathed by the breath, but by Whom the breath breathes, know That alone to be Brahma (the Great), not this which is worshipped (in this world).

Some people believe that Pranaayaama and other forms of breath control will lead us to Him, but these too can only take us thus far and no further.

This is not to say that the study and contemplation of spiritual texts, the chanting of Vedic mantras, Praanaayaama, and other such means have no value whatsoever. Studying this Upanishad itself would become meaningless in that case! No, all these take us to a point where we can subdue our senses enough to be able to take the final leap to reach the Supreme. But before we reach that goal, we reach a 'chasm' that we have to cross all on our own, leaving our body and our senses behind, taking only our Soul on the onward journey. All these practices help us to reach this chasm, and give us some pointers as to how to leap across. This can be compared to doing research after college. It is not as if all the training we received in school and college is meaningless for that research. On the contrary, without it, we would be incapable of looking beyond them! However, doing research itself is a huge leap from the studies we had been pursuing so far. At that point, it becomes fair to say that college will not help you in research. This must be understood as a relative pronouncement and not an absolute one.

The order of the last five verses is most interesting in itself. It represents the reverse order of the development of a human being. As a foetus, the first thing that marks life is Praana. This is followed by the sense of hearing as the foetus starts recognising sounds. Then, the eyes develop and the movement of the eyes is perceived even in the foetus. On birth, the eyes become more developed. As the foetus and, later as the baby, the mind evolves and starts learning about its environment. Lastly, speech develops and the child is able to connect the various sensory inputs with a sequence of sounds.

The Conundrum that is God

After having described how Brahma cannot be attained by the usual means in the previous chapter, the seer now proceeds to clarify the incomprehensibility of God. At the same time, we learn how to discern whether one has realised Brahma or not.

The teacher warns the student –

यदि मन्यसे सुवेदेति दभ्रमेवापि

नूनं त्वं वेत्थ ब्रह्मणो रूपम् ।

यदस्य त्वं यदस्य देवेष्वथ नु

मीमांस्यमेव ते मन्ये विदितम् ॥ २।१ ॥

If you think that you know It well, then you definitely know little of Brahma's form (identity). What you (know) of Its (form, and) what is (known) by the learned ones – I believe that that knowledge should be pondered over by you (i.e., there is more to It than either).

If one feels that she knows Brahma in entirety, then surely there is something lacking in her understanding. Even learned persons cannot know It entirely. The reason for this is simple: God is infinite in every way and the Soul is finite in every way. It is impossible for a finite consciousness to gauge infinity in its entirety. It can comprehend enough to give it a fair idea of that infinity, but an all-encompassing knowledge will surely elude it.

The teacher gives his personal view –

नाहं मन्ये सुवेदेति नो न वेदेति वेद च ।
यो नस्तद्वेद तद्वेद नो न वेदेति वेद च ॥ २।२ ॥

Neither do I think that I know It well, nor do I think I do not know It – this I know. The one among us who (thinks he) knows It, knows It not, (and the one who thinks he) does not know (It, actually) knows (It).

This describes the state of the seeker who has actually 'seen' God, as the teacher explains further –

यस्यामतं तस्य मतं मतं यस्य न वेद सः ।
अविज्ञातं विजानतां विज्ञातमविजानताम् ॥ २।३ ॥

He who (thinks he) does not know (It, actually) knows (It); he who (thinks he) knows (It, actually) does not know (It). (It is) not known by those who (think they) know (It, but is) known by those who do not (think they) know (It).

The three verses put together imply that, when one starts out on the journey of discovering God, it may seem that one has got a grip on what God is all about. But as one proceeds deeper into the field, one discovers that there is much that is unknown, and more importantly, much that cannot *be* known about God. This is something like understanding the inner workings of the Universe. When a child first learns about atoms, everything seems crystal clear, logical and well-arranged: the electrons are spinning round the nucleus of protons and neutrons in well-defined, orderly orbits. But as the same child develops into a physicist, she realises that everything is confused and full of unknowns. Then, she encounters laws like the Heisenberg's Uncertainty Principle that lay down

unambiguously that it is impossible to know everything fully. If this is true of the Material Universe, how much more true it must be in the case of God!

This is not to say that one should stop trying to know Brahma, because the miniscule amount that we can aspire to know about It is good enough to send us into ecstasy, and to give us freedom from Death.

This also defines a characteristic that we should search for in a true Guru – he will never say, 'I know Him well.' If he says that, he does not really know God!

The second line of the next verse is often quoted, but usually used in contexts different from the original intent –

प्रतिबोधविदितं मतममृतत्वं हि विन्दते ।

आत्मना विन्दते वीर्यं विद्यया विन्दतेऽमृतम् ॥ २।४ ॥

(The one who) knows It in the above contradictory fashion attains immortality. Through self(-realisation), one attains power (– the power to reach God). Through knowledge (of God), one attains immortality.

Here, 'Vidyaa' refers to the ultimate knowledge of God.[1]

In the journey towards the realisation of God, one first sees oneself as separate from the body. This gives the Soul tremendous extra-sensory and extra-physical powers described in detail in Patanjali's *Yogadarshanam*. With further sustained effort, one gets a glimpse of God. This overwhelms the Soul into an ecstasy so great that true Yogis hate to come out of their meditation!

The seer now makes an imposing pronouncement that is widely quoted till today –

---

1 The last quarter of the verse – विद्यया विन्दतेऽमृतम् – is often used as a motto by schools. It is a little misplaced because Vidyaa has a different connotation here!

इह चेद्वेदीदथ सत्यमस्ति न चेदिहावेदीन्महती विनष्टिः ।
भूतेषु भूतेषु विचिन्त्य धीराः प्रेत्यास्माल्लोकादमृता भवन्ति ॥ २।५ ॥

If one comes to know (God) here (in this birth itself), then it (the birth) is worthwhile; if one does not come to know (God), then it (the birth) was a great waste[2]. The steadfast ones see (God) in each and every created object. On departing from this world, they become immortals.

'Satya' does not refer to truth here, but to meaningfulness.

Colossal 'waste' happens when the one who has reached so far as to have gained a human birth, after having negotiated many births as other species, then does not achieve the ultimate goal of reaching God. This implies that he would have to restart from at least a few steps behind in the next birth. The next birth is like a reset button and the Soul has to start its struggle from scratch – residing in a mother's womb and learning dedicatedly through childhood, before even thinking of moving further during adulthood. Also, the new birth would bring new hurdles and new pitfalls that threaten its onward progress at every step. Thus, the seer is encouraging the seeker that having come thus far – having gained access to the knowledge of this Upanishad and more – do not lose momentum now; continue with renewed vigour till you reach your final destination – a residence in the Supreme!

Once the Yogi sees God in Samaadhi, he can see It at all times in all things everywhere. It is only then that he can be quite certain that he will attain Moksha after death. All spiritual texts, including the Vedas, *Yogadarshanam*, the Upanishads and the *Bhagawad-geetaa*, mention this same characteristic as revealing impending Moksha.

---

2 *The literal translation is 'a great destruction' – a great destruction of a wonderful opportunity!*

The Parable of the Devas and Brahma

In this chapter, the seer narrates an engaging fable to elucidate the nature of Brahma, which we saw in the previous chapter is crucial to know in order to attain Moksha. We will follow the fable as-is first, and then understand its deeper meaning in the next chapter. These two chapters are entirely in prose.

ब्रह्म ह देवेभ्यो विजिग्ये । तस्य ह ब्रह्मणो विजये देवा अमहीयन्त ।
त ऐक्षन्तास्माकमेवायं विजयोऽस्माकमेवायं महिमेति ॥ ३।१ ॥

Surely (sometime in the distant past), Brahma gained victory for the Devas. In the victory of that Brahma, the Devas became great. (Now) they started thinking that this is our victory and our greatness.

तद्धैषां विजज्ञौ तेभ्यो ह प्रादुर्बभूव तन्न व्यजानत किमिदं यक्षमिति ॥ ३।२ ॥

That (Brahma) came to know about this (thinking of the Devas). (To remove their misconception,) It manifested Itself for them (as a spirit). The Devas could not figure out who this spirit (Yaksha) was.

तेऽग्निमब्रुवञ्जातवेद एतद्विजानीहि किमिदं यक्षमिति तथेति ॥ ३।३ ॥

They said to Agni (the God of Fire and Energy), 'O Jaataveda (another name for fire)! Please find out who this Yaksha is.' Agni replied, 'So be it.'

तदभ्यद्रवत् तमभ्यवदत् कोऽसीत्यग्निर्वा

अहमस्मीत्यब्रवीज्जातवेदा वा अहमस्मीति ॥ ३।४ ॥

(Agni) rushed towards Him. (The Yaksha) asked him, 'Who are you?' (Agni) said (pompously), 'Indeed I am Agni (foremost among all the Devas). Indeed I am Jaataveda (the one found in all created objects).'

तस्मिँस्त्वयि किं वीर्यमिति । अपीदं सर्वं दहेयं यदिदं पृथिव्यामिति ॥ ३।५ ॥

(The Yaksha asked,) 'In that (i.e., the way that you have described yourself), what are your special abilities?' (Agni replied, again egoistically,) 'Indeed, I can burn whatever exists on this earth.'

तस्मै तृणं निदधावेदद्दहेति । तदुपप्रेयाय सर्वजवेन तन्न शशाक दग्धुं स तत

एव निववृते । नैतदशकं विज्ञातुं यदेतद्यक्षमिति ॥ ३।६ ॥

(The Yaksha) kept down a piece of straw for him and said, 'Burn this.' (Agni) approached it (the straw) with all speed, (but) was unable to burn it. (Shamefacedly,) he then returned (to the Devas and told them), 'I was not able to find out who this Yaksha is.'

अथ वायुमब्रुवन् वायवेतद्विजानीहि किमेतद्यक्षमिति तथेति ॥ ३।७ ॥

Then, (the Devas turned to Vaayu, the God of Wind, and) said to him, 'O Vaayu! Please find out who this Yaksha is.' Vaayu replied, 'So be it.'

तदभ्यद्रवत् तमभ्यवदत् कोऽसीति ।

वायुर्वा अहमस्मीत्यब्रवीन्मातरिश्वा वा अहमस्मीति ॥ ३।८ ॥

(Vaayu) rushed towards It. (The Yaksha) said to him, 'Who are

you?' (Vaayu) said (pompously), 'Indeed I am Vaayu (the one that flows). Indeed I am Maatarishvaa (the one that circulates in space).'

तस्मिँस्त्वयि किं वीर्यमिति । अपीदँ सर्वमाददीयं यदिदं पृथिव्यामिति ॥ ३।९ ॥

(The Yaksha asked,) 'In that (i.e., the way that you have described yourself), what are your special abilities?' (Vaayu replied, again egoistically,) 'Indeed, I can lift whatever exists on this earth.'

तस्मै तृणं निदधावेतदादत्स्वेति । तदुपप्रेयाय सर्वजवेन तन्न शशाकादातुं
स तत एव निववृते । नैतदशकं विज्ञातुं यदेतद्यक्षमिति ॥ ३।१० ॥

(The Yaksha) kept down a piece of straw for him and said, 'Lift this.' (Vaayu) approached it (the straw) with all speed, (but) was unable to pick it up. (Shamefacedly,) he then returned (and told the Devas), 'I was not able to find out who this Yaksha is.'

अथेन्द्रमब्रुवन् मघवन्नेतद्विजानीहि किमेतद्यक्षमिति तथेति । तदभ्यद्रवत् ।
तस्मात् तिरोदधे ॥ ३।११ ॥

Then, (the Devas turned to Indra, the Lord of the Devas, and) said to him, 'O Maghavan (the owner of tremendous wealth, both intellectual and Material)! Please find out who this Yaksha is.' Indra replied, 'So be it.' He rushed towards it, (but the Yaksha) disappeared from him.

स तस्मिन्नेवाकाशे स्त्रियमाजगाम बहुशोभमानामुमां
हैमवतीं तां होवाच किमेतद्यक्षमिति ॥ ३।१२ ॥

(Instead) he (Indra) found a woman in that very same place (where the Yaksha had stood) – a woman who was very beautiful, who was Uma (one who 'measures' God) and Haimavatee (loaded with gold ornaments). He asked her, 'Who is this spirit?'

SECTION 4

The Parable Decoded

The fable of the previous chapter ends cryptically in the opening verse of this chapter. The seer then explains the reality and moral behind the parable and gives teachings for the seeker of Brahma in the remaining chapter.

सा ब्रह्मेति होवाच । ब्रह्मणो वा एतद्विजये महीयध्वमिति ।
ततो हैव विदाञ्चकार ब्रह्मेति ॥ ४।१ ॥

She said, 'That was Brahma. All of you (Devas) have attained greatness due to Its victory (not your own, as you mistakenly believe).' It was then that (Indra) came to know that (the Yaksha was) Brahma.

The purport of the story is as follows. Brahma is God; the Devas are the five elements – space (Aakaash), gas (Vaayu), energy (Agni/Teja), liquid (Apa/Jala) and solid (Prthivee); Indra, the lord of the Devas, represents the Soul because it is the lord of its body, which is made up of the five elements (Devas). In the beginning of Creation, Matter lies in an undifferentiated form, called Prakrti. God 'stirs it up' to form the five elements and the amazing properties that they possess, for which they are considered 'divine'.[1] These, in turn,

---

1 *Refer to Introduction, Chart 1: The Order of Creation.*

give rise to all the variety in the Universe, while following laws that cannot be broken by anyone. This is the 'victory' that is mentioned in the first verse of the previous chapter. Seeing the way the Universe functions without any apparent intervention from an external power, it seems that the elements and their amazing properties are sufficient to determine the course of the Universe. Thus, the Devas 'ascribe to themselves' the power to control the Universe. As the elements are themselves inanimate, it is, really speaking, the Soul that starts thinking that there is no God and that the Universe is running of its own accord. Also, it starts thinking that all the actions that it takes and the results that accrue from them have a direct cause-and-effect relationship that cannot be influenced by any other power in any way. That is, the need for divine intervention seems completely unnecessary. An unseen power is easily forgotten…

Under these circumstances, it is imperative for Brahma to ensure that Indra understands the real power behind the Universe, as Indra, the embodied Soul – particularly in the human form – is Its highest creation and It would like Indra to know not only the manifest Universe, but also the hidden reality. The Yaksha, or Brahma, 'revealed' Itself to the Material Devas and showed them that they were powerless without It. Because Indra was the only one capable of actually knowing It, being the only animate Deva, Brahma 'hid' Itself from him. This 'hiding' refers to the very fact mentioned above – the presence of Brahma in the Universe and Its actions can neither be perceived, nor can they be reasoned out easily.

To make Indra aware of Its presence, Brahma revealed the resplendent Uma to him. Uma represents the Vedas. The name itself gives this away, as the word Uma means 'that which allows one to gauge/measure', in this case gauge the Supreme. The Vedas are delightful as much for the knowledge they hold (Uma's beauty), as for the beautiful, embellished poetry they contain (the golden ornaments that Uma wears). The ornaments of Uma also symbolise the 'ornaments' or supernatural powers that the Yogi acquires on understanding the Vedas properly. Thus, it is the Vedas that reveal to the intelligent Soul that there is a Brahma who is behind all the goings-on in this Brahmaanda (Universe). Without the Vedas, it is not really possible to prove unequivocally the existence of God. They are Shabda Pramaanas.[2]

We can now appreciate the beauty of the story, and the very deep message it conveys.[3]

The seer continues –

तस्माद्वा एते देवा अतितरामिवान्यान् देवान् यदग्निर्वायुरिन्द्रस्ते ह्येनन्नेदिष्ठं
पस्पृशुस्ते ह्येनत् प्रथमो विदाञ्चकार ब्रह्मेति ॥ ४।२ ॥

That is why these Devas (Agni, Vayu and Indra) seem to be greater than the others (Aakaash, Jala and Prthivee), because Agni, Vayu and Indra touched this (Brahma) from extremely close and were the first to come to know that It is Brahma.

The importance of Agni and Vayu over the other elements is not very clear. It is possible that this is because Agni represents light and energy, and Vayu movement/change, which form the primary bases of the Universe.

Indra, of course, is far superior to the other divine powers because it is animate and intelligent. It is also able to control and manipulate the others to a limited extent. This is emphasised in the next sentence –

तस्माद्वा इन्द्रोऽतितरामिवान्यान् देवान् स ह्येनन्नेदिष्ठं पस्पर्श स ह्येनत्
प्रथमो विदाञ्चकार ब्रह्मेति ॥ ४।३ ॥

(Also,) that is why Indra is greater than all the other Devas,

---

2 *Refer to Introduction, point 10.*
3 *Due to the influence of the Puraanas, sometimes these Devas are interpreted as animate beings living in a higher sphere called Heaven, and controlling the corresponding elements on Earth. However, this is only a mythological construct. The divinity of the Devas, or elements, lies only in the unique powers they are imbued with, the special properties they have.*

(because) indeed he touched this (Brahma) from extremely close and he was the very first to know Brahma.

Here is proclaimed the greatness of Indra, not only over Aakaash, Jala and Prthivee, but also over Agni and Vayu. Being the Soul, Indra is actually the only one among the Devas that can actually know God. Therefore, it is far superior to inanimate Matter.

The above two sentences are also interesting in that they seem to be contradictory in the way that we understand language today. However, this is a typical construct in ancient texts, and is sometimes interpreted incorrectly these days.

तस्यैष आदेशो यदेतद्विद्युतो व्यद्युतदा इतीन्यमीमिषदा इत्यधिदैवतम् ॥ ४।४ ॥

It is Brahma's command because of which this electricity sparks, or, (the eye) blinks. This is the facet (of this Brahmee Vidyaa, the knowledge of Brahma) that is related to the Devas (Adhidaivata).

There are three aspects to anything in this world – that related to the Material world (Aadhidaivika), that related to other beings (Aadhibhautika) and that related to the spirit, i.e., oneself, one's body or God (Aadhyatmika). Thus, earthquakes and other natural or accidental happenings are covered under Aadhidaivika. Cruelty, kindness, etc., towards other creatures comes under Aadhibhautika. Illness, ignorance, knowledge, etc., of one's own is Aadhyaatmika. In the above verse, classifying the blinking of an eye (even though Aadhyaatmika) as Aadhidaivika and juxtaposing it with electricity, seems to suggest that the electrical nature of the command for blinking was recognised by the ancients. Electricity being part of Nature, this aspect of Brahma is Aadhidaivika.[4]

Each and every thing that happens in this world happens at the command of the Supreme. If He does not ordain it, then even a leaf cannot sway in the breeze. Thus, all the Devas are under the

---

4 *Similarly, disease and other things caused by other beings may be considered Aadhibhautika at a deeper level. Thus, at a deeper level, some items may move from one class to another.*

supreme command of the Lord. The fact that they seem to behave most consistently is only an aspect of the Lord Himself – He is the one who is systematic, consistent and orderly; He is the one who sets up laws that are immutable. Order is a sign of intelligence, and the beautiful and extremely complex order of the Universe is a reflection of a higher intelligence.[5] Just like a house does not get constructed on its own, so also, life has not originated on Earth on its own. Scientists are only now discovering how many things came together to create this blue planet called Earth and all the life it sustains. They call it the Goldilocks Effect. Did all that happen by chance? The astute reader should contemplate on this fact.

The question raised at the beginning of the Upanishad is now answered explicitly –

अथाध्यात्मं यदेतद्गच्छतीव च मनोऽनेन चैतदुपस्मरत्यभीक्ष्णँ सङ्कल्पः ॥ ४।५ ॥

Now for the spiritual aspect (Adhyaatma[6]) – this seeming movement of the mind (referred to in verse 1/1) is due to This (Brahma), and because of It, the mind remembers and determines to act.

Regarding the relationship of the body and the spirit, i.e., in the spiritual context, we may feel quite certain that the body is under our control. However, the Upanishad declares that each and every movement of the body is also dependent on Brahma in the ultimate analysis. While we do have superficial control of the mind, and through it on the body, it is by the Lord's permission that we perform the smallest of actions or think the simplest of thoughts. Just as the great Agni and Vaayu lost all their powers in front of the Yaksha, so also the physical body can lose all its powers in an instant, if the Lord so ordains. We should remember this fact and not gloat over the greatness we achieve in this world – this is one of the teachings of the parable.

---

5 *The Law of Entropy may seem to buck this trend, but if it is a law, then we have to accept that it specifies order in the chaos!*
6 *Refer to the previous verse for explanation.*

Here, the mind, even though it is part of the Material body, is considered to be related to the Soul, because it is deeply linked to the Soul and is its primary contact with the body. In the same manner, anything related to the body is typically covered under Adhyaatma.

तद्ध तद्वनं नाम तद्वनमित्युपासितव्यं स य एतदेवं वेदाभि हैनं
सर्वाणि भूतानि संवाञ्छन्ति ॥ ४।६ ॥

That (Brahma) is known as 'Tadvana' (as It is the most desirable, the ultimate goal of life). Therefore, It should be worshipped as Tadvana. The one who knows It as such, all beings will want (love) him similarly.

The root 'Van' means 'to ask for/desire', 'to honour/worship/ serve', 'to experience' or 'to sound'. Other than the last meaning, all meanings apply to Brahma here, as the Soul should desire It, worship it and experience It. Keeping all these meanings in mind, the sage recommends that Brahma be called Tadvana by the seeker, to remind himself that he is under the control of Brahma at all times, and that Brahma is his ultimate goal.

Many legends abound about how even the fiercest of animals do not harm the enlightened ones; indeed, they are friendly towards them. Similarly, people seek the company of enlightened ones to guide them towards the path of righteousness. This friendliness is because the enlightened Soul does not possess any malice towards any other being; indeed, it is benevolent towards all animate beings and inanimate things. The enlightened Soul itself becomes like God in that respect.

The teacher draws the Upanishad to a close –

उपनिषदं भो ब्रूहीत्युक्ता त उपनिषद्ब्राह्मीं वाव त उपनिषदमब्रूमेति ॥ ४।७॥

(The teacher says,) '(You, the student, had requested,) "Please

preach to me about Brahma." That teaching of Brahma has now been delivered. Verily, I have told the Upanishad to you.'

Having delivered the sermon about the nature of Brahma and Its relationship to the individual Soul and the inanimate Matter making up this Universe, the seer now gives the tools to find Brahma in a nutshell – a very loaded nutshell indeed! –

तस्यै तपो दमः कर्मेति प्रतिष्ठा वेदाः सर्वाङ्गानि सत्यमायतनम् ॥ ४।८॥

For this (Braahmee Vidyaa), physical austerities (Tapa), mental austerities (Dama) and righteous deeds (Karma) are the bases, Vedas are the limbs and truth is its abode.

These same three bases are mentioned in Yogadarshanam as Karma Yoga, comprising Tapa, Swaadhyaaya and Eeshwarapranidhaana,[7] meaning physical austerity, self-study of scriptures and surrendering one's deeds to God, respectively. If you ponder over it, you will realise how the two teachings correspond.

To become a candidate for Braahmee Vidyaa, one has to ensure that she does not commit a wrongful act through thought, speech or action. She must guard against every wrong act by continuous vigilance and self-control.

To 'touch' Braahmee Vidyaa, one must understand her limbs – the Vedas. Note again how much importance seer after seer places on the Vedas. It is only in the last 2000 years or so that the focus has shifted to meditation, and sometimes also, service to the Guru or society in general. Knowledge, particularly of the Vedas, has been placed on the back burner because most preachers have never even set their eyes on them! The Vedas are difficult texts and a lot of study goes into understanding them, even when their commentaries are read; and the commentaries prevalent today mostly suffer from incongruencies and errors.

---

7 तपःस्वाध्यायेश्वरप्रणिधानानि क्रियायोगः ॥ योगदर्शनम् २।१॥

Truth is of primary importance if you have to find Brahma. There are many attractive diversions on the path of life. If you decide to take one of those, rest assured that you will never reach Brahma. Just as once the knowledge of the Earth being round was lost, it took many centuries and many people's effort to rediscover it, so also, in this non-obvious pursuit of Brahma, many 'easy and obvious paths' will be shown to you and you will fritter away your precious time on this planet in fruitless endeavours.

The Path of Truth is long and arduous, but the rewards more than make up for the journey, as the following Vaidika Mantra confirms –

ऋतस्य हि शुरुधः सन्ति पूर्वीर्-
ऋतस्य धीतिर्वृजनानि हन्ति ।
ऋतस्य श्लोको बधिरा ततर्द
कर्णा बुधानः शुचमान आयोः ॥ ऋक्० ४।२३।८॥

The armies of truth are ancient. The knowledge of truth destroys sinful behavior. The words of truth tear open deaf ears, leading to enlightenment and purification of one's life.

The verse implies that truth is powerful, it cannot be suppressed. Life can be purified by knowing the truth. That is why seekers go after it. Not only should knowledge be sought out, but once found, it should be transmitted to benefit other human beings as well. The purification provided by truth will ultimately lead to salvation.

There are various sects and cults today that indulge in unholy behaviour. This happens when we take recourse to even a single untruth, because one lie leads to another and another till we are left standing on a mountain of lies...

यो वा एतामेवं वेदापहत्य पाप्मानमनन्ते स्वर्गे लोके ज्येये
लोके प्रतितिष्ठति प्रतितिष्ठति ॥ ४।९॥

The one who understands (Brahma) as such (as described above), destroying his sins, becomes established firmly in the eternal supreme abode of bliss.

This is the Phala-shruti describing what lies in store for the seeker of Brahma. It reminds the seeker why she is undertaking this arduous journey, lest she starts flagging on the way. It is like a pep talk by the leader of the expedition at Camp 4 of Mount Everest to the climber ready to summit!

With this final word of encouragement, the Upanishad draws to a close.

Death and the Boy
Kathopanishad

CONTENTS

Introduction to Kathopanishad ... 77

Chapter 1: At Death's Door ... 79

Section I: Nachiketaa Meets Yama ... 79

Section II: The Two Paths in Life ... 99

Section III: Finding The Ultimate ... 121

Chapter 2: God and the Soul ... 137

Section I: The Nature of God ... 137

Section II: The Soul ... 149

Section III: The Tree of the World ... 161

Introduction to Kathopanishad

The Katha Upanishad is probably the most popular of the Upanishads, largely because it contains the heart-warming story of the curious boy Nachiketaa and his encounter with his Guru – death, personified as Yama. But this is not the only reason for its popularity – its verses express the teaching so succinctly and in verses that are so lyrical, that they have been copied in toto, or in a slightly modified format, in many other spiritual texts, e.g., the *Bhagawad-geetaa*. In fact, some teachers opine that the Geetaa is really a commentary on Kathopanishad! The reader, too, will find many verses that appeal to her and would be compelled to include them in her daily prayers, or Sandhyaa.

Kathopanishad comes under the **Krshna branch of the Yajurveda**. As mentioned in the Introduction, each Upanishad is linked to a Veda, and more often than not, to a particular school of the Veda. Thus, we have texts available for the two schools of the Yajurveda – Shukla (white) Yajurveda and Krshna (black) Yajurveda. This Upanishad falls under Krshna Yajurveda, and belongs to the **Katha shaakhaa** (branch), i.e., the school of thought propounded by Rshi Katha. Thus, in effect, Rshi Katha is the author of this Upanishad.

Kathopanishad consists of two chapters with three sections each. These sections are called 'Vallee', meaning a creeper. This is a poetic description for something that takes us upwards! Sometimes, the Upanishad is split up directly as six Vallees without any chapter demarcation. The total number of verses is 29+25+17+15+15+18= 119. Most verses are in the Trishtup Chhanda (a particular Vaidika poetic metre), though other formats like Anushtup and even prose formats are found.

Some commentators speak of Katha (कठ) Upanishad as Kathaa (कथा) Upanishad. While this obviously reflects the ignorance of the speaker/writer, it is a sign of our times that today people do not know enough to be able to correct this misconception and reject such teaching based on this basic lack of knowledge.

CHAPTER ONE

At Death's Door

Section I: Nachiketaa Meets Yama

The Upanishad begins with the story of Nachiketaa, grabbing the reader's interest from the very outset. The fact that the story is still retold today in all kinds of formats bears testimony to its endearing quality. This is because we can relate to Nachiketaa's predicament even today.

While the story appears to be a part of history, it is in fact an imaginary tale and its meaning is built up in the very names of the *dramatis personae*. Thus, Nachiketaa is derived from the root 'Chikit' meaning Gati, i.e., knowledge, attainment and movement. The 'Na' prefix stands for negation of these qualities. Thus, Nachiketaa stands for the Soul that is ignorant, has not attained Brahma and is rooted in its body, or, is the unchanging component in the body. How beautifully the relevant characteristics of the Soul are encoded in this pleasing word! His father's name Vaajashravaa is also full of meaning. It stands for a person whose wealth is food or worldly knowledge, thus implying the wealthy or worldly-wise family background of Nachiketaa. It is easy to acquire wealth and fame in this world; but in spiritual terms, one will still be considered ignorant and needy – in need of spiritual wealth! Death is called Yama in the

Upanishad, which stands for quieting or bringing to an end, serving food, controlling and giving. These meanings apply to this story as follows: Yama quietens the perturbed Nachiketaa, brings his life to an end, serves him spiritual succour, controls life and death of beings, and gives spiritual knowledge to Nachiketaa. God (Brahma) Himself has all these properties and is referred to as such in the Vedas. Thus, **the Upanishad really represents a dialogue between the Soul and Brahma.** This is why these names have been selected in this Upanishad – not to describe some historical event! In fact, the story itself is quite mythical and unnatural and should be understood merely as an interesting frame in which to impart the message.

उशन् ह वै वाजश्रवसः सर्ववेदसं ददौ ।
तस्य ह नचिकेता नाम पुत्र आस ॥१।१।१॥

It is well known that, once upon a time, desiring (release from worldly attachments and the sorrow they entail), Vaajashravaa gave away all his possessions (as part of the Vishwajit or Sarwamedha Yajna). He had a son by the name of Nachiketaa.

The Sarwamedha Yajna is a well-known Yajna (fire-sacrifice) of ancient India. Typically, a king would perform this Yajna and give away all he possessed to the poor and the needy. Very often he was left with nothing but the clothes on his back. Not only was this done to assist the needy, this was also a means by which the king ensured that he was not attached to any of his possessions. This step is of great significance as it opens the doors to salvation and freedom from the sorrows of life and death.

Vaajashravaa is not portrayed as a king here, but as a wealthy Braahmana.

As was the custom in those days, Vaajashravaa had many names that appear later in the Upanishad. Thus, he was also called Uddaalaka, which could be modified to Auddaalaki (verse 1|1|11), as well. His father's name was Aruna. So, he was also called Aaruni (verse 1|1|11). He was of the clan of Gotama; so, he was called Gautama (verse 1|1|10).

तँ ह कुमारँ सन्तं दक्षिणासु नीयमानासु श्रद्धाविवेश सोऽमन्यत ॥१।१।२॥

It is also well known that, as the donations (in the form of cows) were being taken away (by the recipients), a sense of righteousness entered the young boy. He thought (continued in the next sentence)...

This is the only description of Nachiketaa that is afforded to us by the Upanishad – that he was a Kumaara, a young lad, probably a teenager, though it could possibly refer to a younger boy as well.

The usage of the word 'Shraddhaa' is of significance here. Today, the word has only one meaning – faith, usually referring to blind faith. However, the word arises from two roots – Shrat = truth; and Dhaa = to uphold/bear. Thus, belief in that which upholds the truth or represents truth is called Shraddhaa – somewhat the opposite of blind faith! Such a sense of truthfulness and justice entered Nachiketaa's mind.

He mused –

पीतोदका जग्धतृणा दुग्धदोहा निरिन्द्रियाः ।
अनन्दा नाम ते लोकास्तान् स गच्छति ता ददत् ॥१।१।३॥

These (cows) have had their last fill of water; they have eaten their last morsel of grass; they have been milked for the final time (they are too old to give milk any more); their senses are weak. Surely, the person who gives (such a worthless gift) attains a life that lacks happiness.

In India, the Law of Karma[1] runs deep in the ethos. That is what is being referred to here: one may give a worthless donation, but surely the consequence of this deed has to be future unhappiness rather than the happiness that the donor – in this case, his father – seeks. He is

---

1 *See Introduction, point 6.*

giving away cows that are old and infirm, and should be justly retired.

Again, in India, the cow has been held deeply sacred among all the animals since time immemorial. This is particularly due to her milk, which is nutritious for Man in both youth and old age. The cow's milk is next only to mother's milk in importance. For this reason, just as the mother is revered, so is the cow. The donating of cows is said to bring great auspiciousness to the donor. However, this cannot be said to hold true when the cows being donated are not worth a dime!

'Loka' refers to the place one is born in, such as the Earth. The word arises from the root 'Lokr' meaning to see or speak. So, all species where the Soul 'sees', i.e., encounters the results of its past deeds, or speaks a language as a mortal being, are Lokas in Yaugika terms.[2] 'Naama' used here in conjunction with 'Loka' does not imply 'a place called Ananda', but rather 'surely'; and Ananda is an adjective of Loka, meaning births that entail more sorrow than happiness.

Trying to gently bring this to his father's notice, Nachiketaa addresses him –

स होवाच पितरं तत कस्मै मां दास्यसीति ।
द्वितीयं तृतीयं तँ होवाच मृत्यवे त्वा ददामीति ॥ १। १। ४॥

He said to his father, 'O Father! To whom will you give me?' (The father ignored the question. So, Nachiketaa) asked him a second and third time. (Annoyed, the father said,) 'I give you to Death!'

Nachiketaa's question implied that since you seem to be giving away everything – even that which should not be given because it is useless – probably you want to give me away, too, who am yet young and not of much use to anybody as of now.

Being of a serious disposition, Nachiketaa takes his father's words at face value and wonders –

---

2 See Introduction, Explanatory Note on Vaidika Words.

बहूनामेमि प्रथमो बहूनामेमि मध्यमः ।
किंस्विद्यमस्य कर्तव्यं यन्मयाद्य करिष्यति ॥ १ । १ । ५ ॥

I am ahead of many, and among many I am medium (but I am really not placed last anywhere). What is the work required by Yama, which (my father) will accomplish through me today?

Nachiketaa feels that he was never a laggard at any job assigned to him. So, there is no reason for his father to want to get rid of him. Therefore, it must be that his father wants to accomplish some purpose of Yama, the Lord of Death, and is sending him to his death to achieve that.

The father now presumably sees his son get ready to obey his command and repents. However, going back on one's words was considered a sin in that bygone era, and Nachiketaa would not allow his father's words to go unfulfilled. He consoles his father with wisdom far beyond his years –

अनुपश्य यथा पूर्वे प्रतिपश्य तथापरे ।
सस्यमिव मर्त्यः पच्यते सस्यमिवाजायते पुनः ॥ १ । १ । ६ ॥

Look back at how our forefathers (have been), and similarly, see now the others (i.e., those present today). Mortals ripen like crop and, like crop, they grow back again.

Nachiketaa tells his father, 'Don't cry over me and don't incur sin by going against your words, because anyway I have to die someday, just as our forefathers have done and just as later generations will. My time has come today, that is all. New generations will arrive, just as crops grow back, and my presence will hardly be noticed. Revel in them and forget about me.'

Somehow the father agrees to send Nachiketaa to Yama and somehow the deed is done. Nachiketaa arrives at the door of Yama, but Yama is out of town. His wife receives him, but he refuses to accept any food or water. On Yama's return, his wife pleads with him –

वैश्वानरः प्रविशत्यतिथिर्ब्राह्मणो गृहान् ।
तस्यैताँ शान्तिं कुर्वन्ति हर वैवस्वतोदकम् ॥१।१।७॥

O Vaivasvata (Son of the Sun)! The Fire-god Agni himself enters the homes (of householders[3] in the form of) a Braahmana guest. They pacify him (with Arghya=water to wash the hands and face, Paadya=water to wash the feet, Aasana=a comfortable seat, etc.). You also take this water (to pacify Nachiketaa).

This reveals that Nachiketaa was indeed a Braahmana and, even though he was young, Braahmanas, as the repositories of Vaidika knowledge, were to be treated with the utmost respect.

Arghya, Paadya, Aasana, water to drink, etc. were the minimum courtesies to be extended to a guest, weary from the road as he was. Even today, this practice continues in India, though mostly in a reduced format, and the guest is always welcomed with water even in commercial establishments.

The wife continues to remind Yama of the calamities that befall a householder who does not welcome the Braahmana at his door –

आशाप्रतीक्षे संगतँ सूनृतां च
इष्टापूर्ते पुत्रपशूँश्च सर्वान् ।
एतद्वृङ्क्ते पुरुषस्याल्पमेधसो
यस्यानश्नन् वसति ब्राह्मणो गृहे ॥१।१।८॥

The Braahmana who resides unattended in the house of a feeble-minded person destroys all the fortune that is due in the long term and the short, (as a result of following Dhaarmika precepts dutifully, such as) good company, honest and sweet speech, performance of Yajnas and charitable acts (such as building hospitals for the poor), also the

---

3 See Introduction, point 11.

family and all the animals (and other kinds of Material wealth that one is currently enjoying).

The verse lays down some of the fundamental principles of Vaidika life. Firstly, it lays down the Law of Karma[4], which ordains that when one has followed one's Dharma (duty, righteousness, ethics), one obtains wealth and happiness. For the householder, this amounts to a family full of children and wealth in the form of belongings, of which animals such as cows, horses, donkeys, dogs, etc., formed a significant part in yesteryears. Thus the term 'Putra-pashoon'. This constitutes the current fortune. But fortune is also awaited in the long term (Aashaa) and the short term (Prateekshaa). This is because good deeds have already been performed and now their results are expected.

The verse specifies that good, or Dhaarmika, deeds consist of:

- Good company (Sangata) – It usually includes our efforts to learn about Vaidika Dharma through people learned in such precepts, also called Satsanga. However, it also includes the honest job that we do regularly, with people who are engaged in a Dhaarmika means of livelihood.

- Sweet speech (Soonrtaa) – harsh words should be avoided to the extent possible. They hurt the other even more than physical abuse.

- Altruistic deeds for society, animals and the environment – these include Ishta Karma, meaning the performance of Yajnas (loosely, the fire-sacrifice) that cleans up toxins from the environment and brings happiness to all living beings; and Aapoorta Karma, which includes other munificent acts like building wells, hospitals, gardens, etc., for the benefit of both humans and animals.

Having practised self-control and performed the above-mentioned auspicious deeds, it is justifiable to look forward to the promised

____
4 *Refer to Introduction, point 6.*

returns. Thus, a good job will yield honest wealth, good company will improve knowledge and encourage sticking to the straight and narrow path, sweet speech, Ishta and Aapoorta deeds will increase the happiness quotient of all around us, returning to us also as such.

While it is an exaggeration that all these will be lost if the Braahmana is not catered to, the statement highlights how much the care of a guest (Atithee-sevaa) was, and still is, important in the Indian ethos.

Following his wife's advice, Yama takes the water to Nachiketaa, and goes a step further to say –

तिस्रो रात्रीर्यदवात्सीर्गृहे

अनश्नन् ब्रह्मन्नतिथिर्नमस्यः ।

नमस्तेऽस्तु ब्रह्मन् स्वस्ति मेऽस्तु

तस्मात् प्रति त्रीन् वरान् वृणीष्व ॥१।१।९॥

O Brahman, the learned one! You are a revered guest and I bow to you. O Brahman! Bless me with good fortune! For the three nights that you have stayed at my house without any food, please accept three boons (i.e., one for each night).

Of course, the Lord of Death who grants boons to others does not need any blessings from the receiver of boons! However, this is just a story that engages and reflects the norms of that yesteryear society while doing so. Those norms included tremendous humility before the learned.

Nachiketaa is no simpleton. In the very first boon, he asks for many things at once! –

शान्तसंकल्पः सुमना यथा स्याद्वीतमन्युर्गौतमो माभि मृत्यो ।

त्वत्प्रसृष्टं माभिवदेत् प्रतीत एतत्त्रयाणां प्रथमं वरं वृणे ॥१।१।१०॥

O Death! As the first of the three boons, I choose that when I am sent back by you, may my father recognise me and speak kindly to me.

May my father (Uddaalaka) of the clan of Gotama be peaceful, happy to see me and rid of his anger towards me.

Can you count the number of things Nachiketaa has asked for here? Here are some of them –

1. I should return from death to the Land of the Living.

2. I should return to the same family as the same boy that I was.

3. My father, and my family in general, should not see me as a ghost and accept it as a natural course of events that I, who was dead, am now alive once again.

4. They should recognise me and not perceive me as an imposter.

5. They should not become excited by this course of events.

6. My father should, however, lose the anger towards me that I had left him with, and welcome me with open arms.

Yama has no problems in acquiescing –

यथा पुरस्ताद्द्रविता प्रतीत

औद्दालकिरारुणिर्मत्प्रसृष्टः ।

सुखँ रात्रीः शयिता वीतमन्युस्-

त्वां दृष्टशिवान् मृत्युमुखात् प्रमुक्तम् ॥१।१।११॥

Seeing you released from the mouth of Death, Auddaalaki Aaruni (Nachiketaa's father)[5] will be induced by me to recognise you as before and, devoid of his anger, he will sleep well in the nights (of his remaining life, i.e., he will not have any misgivings about your unnatural return).

Yama plays along and grants all the wishes that Nachiketaa asked for. In reality, nobody can return from the dead.

Nachiketaa now asks for the second boon –

---

5 *Refer to verse 1/1/1 for the various names of Nachiketaa's father.*

स्वर्गे लोके न भयं किंचनास्ति

न तत्र त्वं न जरया बिभेति ।

उभे तीर्त्वाशनायापिपासे

शोकातिगो मोदते स्वर्गलोके ॥१।१।१२॥

In Heaven (Swarga Loka), there is no fear of any kind, there is no you (i.e., death), nor is there fear of old age. One goes beyond both hunger and thirst, and having gone past sorrow (of all kinds), revels in Swarga Loka.

In fact, there is no separate place called Swarga, or Heaven; a human birth with minimal sorrows is itself Heaven. All people living lives with a preponderance of joy and a lack of sorrows should consider themselves blessed and to be Souls who have done good deeds in their previous birth(s).

Continuing, Nachiketaa says –

स त्वमग्निँ स्वर्ग्यमध्येषि मृत्यो

प्रब्रूहि त्वँ श्रद्दधानाय मह्यम् ।

स्वर्गलोका अमृतत्वं भजन्त

एतद्द्वितीयेन वृणे वरेण ॥१।१।१३॥

O Death! Please preach to me, who am desirous of knowing the truth (about Heaven), about the fire-sacrifice (Yajna) by means of which one attains Swarga, (as) Souls residing in Swarga Loka enjoy immortality. This is what I choose as my second boon.

Nachiketaa says that one attains immortality by performing a Yajna. These are conflicting statements that do not agree with the rest of the text. In fact, fire sacrifices yield Punya[6] which translate into future joys. They can never lead to immortality or emancipation from the Cycle of Life and Death, called Moksha, as the author will himself say later in the Upanishad.

6 See Introduction, point 6.

Yama again complies readily –

प्र ते ब्रवीमि तदु मे निबोध
स्वर्ग्यमग्निं नचिकेतः प्रजानन् ।
अनन्तलोकाप्तिमथो प्रतिष्ठां
विद्धि त्वमेतं निहितं गुहायाम् ॥१।१।१३॥

O Nachiketaa! Knowing full well this Swarga-yielding fire-sacrifice, I now teach it to you. Learn it well from me. Know that this knowledge provides access to eternal Lokas (of happiness), is their basis, and is hidden in the recesses (of the intellect).

Yama's heart is gladdened to have a Shishya, a student, who asks all the right questions and then listens to his every word with the keenest attention. What else does a good teacher desire?! The Vedas themselves enjoin the scholar to share his/her knowledge with the right student at the earliest.[7]

He proceeds to fulfil his promise –

लोकादिमग्निं तमुवाच तस्मै
या इष्टका यावतीर्वा यथा वा ।
स चापि तत् प्रत्यवदद्यथोक्त-
मथास्य मृत्युः पुनरेवाह तुष्टः ॥१।१।१५॥

Death told him (Nachiketaa) that knowledge of the fire-sacrifice (Yajna), which is the basis of attaining Swarga Loka, including how many of which bricks (were to be used) and how they were to be arranged (in the construction of the altar). He (Nachiketaa), too, repeated all that was said, exactly as it was said. This satisfied Death and he said further – (continued in the next verse)

Yajnas are powerful environment-cleansers. They remove

---

7 प्र तद्द्रोचेदमृतं नु विद्वान् ... ॥यजुर्वेदः ३२।९॥

toxins from a large area and, thus, bring relief to all creatures in the vicinity. This provides immense good credit (Punya) to the one conducting the sacrifice. In the future, the Soul redeems this Punya[8] for a joyful and fulfilling life. Many types of fire-sacrifices are described in texts called the Shrauta Granthas. Yama seems to be preaching a powerful one among them.

For a teacher, nothing gives more joy than a student who has imbibed his teaching perfectly. Filled to the brim with this satisfaction, Yama grants another boon to Nachiketaa –

तमब्रवीत् प्रीयमाणो महात्मा

वरं तवेहाद्य ददामि भूयः ।

तवैव नाम्ना भवितायमग्निः

सृङ्कां चेमामनेकरूपां गृहाण ॥१।१।१६॥

Thoroughly pleased (with Nachiketaa's recital), the great Soul (Yama) told him (Nachiketaa), 'Now, I grant you one more boon – this Yajna will henceforth be known by your name. Also, take this necklace of many forms.

We will learn a little more about this fire-sacrifice in the verses that follow, and infer what it could imply, as no such Yajna is referred to in any of the known texts.

In olden days, men wore almost as much jewellery as women. Even renunciates would wear a necklace or two, as is very often seen among the Saadhus even today. Thus, Yama's gift to Nachiketaa is appropriate indeed.

Yama further elaborates on the benefits of the fire-sacrifice –

त्रिणाचिकेतस्त्रिभिरेत्य सन्धिं

त्रिकर्मकृत् तरति जन्ममृत्यू ।

ब्रह्मजज्ञं देवमीड्यं विदित्वा

निचाय्येमाँ शान्तिमत्यन्तमेति ॥१।१।१७॥

---

8 See Introduction, point 6.

(Whosoever) performs the Naachiketa Yajna in three ways, combining the performance with the three (Vedas – Rg, Yaju, Saama) and having performed the three types of deeds (Yajna, Daana, Tapa), goes beyond birth and death (i.e., achieves Moksha). Knowing the Divine Lord, who knows all in this Universe created by Brahma (i.e., Himself), by performing (this sacrifice, that person) attains extreme peace.

The householder[9] is supposed to maintain three types of fires burning at all times in different parts of the house. These are called Aahvaneeya, Gaarhapatya and Daakshinaagni. These are probably the three fires referred to by the word 'Tri-naachiketa'.[10]

These fires or fire-sacrifices must be combined with the knowledge and chanting of Vaidika hymns. The Vedas are given as three in number here. This does not mean that the Atharva-veda is not a Veda. When the Vedas are described as three in number, it is to be understood as follows: all metric compositions (Padya or verses) are called Rg; all non-metric compositions (Gadya or plain text) are called Yaju; all compositions that are to be sung are called Saama. In ancient India, names were very flexible objects and were not as hard and fast as they are today. Many names could refer to one object, and many objects could be referred to by one name!

Knowledge of the Vedas is important not only to chant during the sacrifice, but also to understand Dharma (righteousness). Only a righteous person can expect to attain Swarga Loka. Also, the Vedas provide information on Brahma, whom it is important to know for enlightenment.

The three types of deeds that are important for attaining happiness are mentioned in Chhaandogya Upanishad,[11] viz., Yajna, Daana and Tapa. Yajnas are important to gain Punya as they are beneficial for the environment and all beings in the vicinity, as

---

9 See Introduction, point 11.

10 It is also possible that this word refers to a particular Yajna called 'Naachiketa' which is to be performed thrice. However, the next verse supports the above meaning better.

11 त्रयो धर्मस्कन्धा यज्ञोऽध्ययनं दानमिति ॥ छान्दोग्योपनिषत्, प्रपाठक २, खण्ड २३, प्रवाक् १॥

we saw earlier. Daana, or donation, involves not only money, food, clothes, etc., but also knowledge. In fact, knowledge-donation was considered the most precious by ancient Indians. Tapa, or austerities, involves tolerating dualities, such as heat and cold, hunger and thirst, etc. These need not be self-imposed, the idea being to be able to handle the vagaries of Nature and circumstances without breaking down and committing a sin. These three acts together open the doorway to happiness in this and the after-life, or Swarga Loka.

The rewards of performing the above actions are further elaborated in this verse –

त्रिणाचिकेतस्त्रयमेतद्विदित्वा
य एवं विद्वाँश्चिनुते नाचिकेतम् ।
स मृत्युपाशान् पुरतः प्रणोद्य
शोकातिगो मोदते स्वर्गलोके ॥१।१।१८॥

Knowing this triad of Trinaachiketa Yajnas, the one who performs the Naachiketa sacrifice, destroying the snares of death in this life itself, he goes beyond sorrow and delights in Swarga Loka.

The performance of the sacrifice provides a sure-shot way to happiness in this and the after-life. Again, this must be taken allegorically, rather than literally.

Yama now asks Nachiketaa to ask for the third boon –

एष तेऽग्निर्नचिकेतः स्वर्ग्यो
यमवृणीथा द्वितीयेन वरेण ।
एतमग्निं तवैव प्रवक्ष्यन्ति जनासस्-
तृतीयं वरं नचिकेतो वृणीष्व ॥१।१।१९॥

O Nachiketaa! This Swarga-yielding Agni that I have described to you, which you had asked for through your second boon, shall henceforth be called by your name by people. (Now,) O Nachiketaa, choose your third boon.

Assuring him of eternal fame for setting the ideal among students, Yama now urges Nachiketaa to allow him to make good his third promise.

Nachiketaa has reserved the best for the last –

येयं प्रेते विचिकित्सा मनुष्ये-

ऽस्तीत्येके नायमस्तीति चैके ।

एतद्विद्यामनुशिष्टस्त्वयाहं

वराणामेष वरस्तृतीयः ॥१।१।२०॥

There is this doubt on the death of a person – some say that he continues to exist and others say he does not. I would like to be taught this by you, (so that I may make a determination on this matter). This is the third of the boons (that I choose).

This question seems a bit misplaced at this juncture, as Nachiketaa's and Yama's description of Swarga Loka was of a realm where the Soul was free of birth and death, and they have just finished describing a Yajna to release the Soul from Material bondage. Some commentators have indeed called Swarga Moksha or salvation, though I have been careful to call it 'a happy life in this birth and the next', since the way to Moksha is yet to be described. Either interpretation, however, implies that the Soul continues to exist after death to enjoy such a realm. Even more curiously, Nachiketaa is himself dead at this juncture and presumably only his Soul has reached Yamaraaja! These contradictions reveal very clearly that this story is just that – a story to engage the reader. It has no historical content, is full of contradictions and should under no circumstances be mistaken for the truth. The real sermon starts from the next section.

Yama hesitates to fulfil this boon. He says –

देवैरत्रापि विचिकित्सितं पुरा
न हि सुविज्ञेयमणुरेष धर्मः ।
अन्यं वरं नचिकेतो वृणीष्व
मा मोपरोत्सीरति मा सृजैनम् ॥१।१।२१॥

Even the Devas (extremely learned scholars) have earlier had doubts in this matter. This extremely subtle Dharma (property, subject) is indeed not easy to understand. O Nachiketaa! Choose another boon. Do not force me. Release me (from this request)!

The existence of the immortal Soul seems to be too difficult a subject for Yama to transmit to Nachiketaa! Be that as it may, this conversation also has something to teach in the following verses. Yama's answer in the following chapters does not really answer this question, taking it for granted, and covers much deeper subjects.

Nachiketaa reveals his quick-wittedness once again –

देवैरत्रापि विचिकित्सितं किल
त्वं च मृत्यो यन्न सुविज्ञेयमात्थ ।
वक्ता चास्य त्वादृगन्यो न लभ्यो
नान्यो वरस्तुल्य एतस्य कश्चित् ॥१।१।२२॥

O Death! Even the Devas had doubts on this subject, right? And you yourself are saying that it is not easy to comprehend. Then, another teacher like you is not possible to obtain. (Surely,) there is no other boon that is equivalent to this one!

As Nachiketaa has revealed before, he is a hard one to put off by mere words. He displays a confidence and a perseverance to achieve what he sets out to do. Wisely, he realises that if even the learned have doubts, and Yama knows the answer, then he is a rare breed, and he cannot allow this opportunity to understand from him to pass.

Yama tries to tempt him with worldly wealth –

शतायुषः पुत्रपौत्रान् वृणीष्व
बहून् पशून् हस्तिहिरण्यमश्वान् ।
भूमेर्महदायतनं वृणीष्व
स्वयं च जीव शरदो यावदिच्छसि ॥ १।१।२३॥

Accept many offspring and many of their offspring who will each live for a hundred years or more, many animals, elephants, gold and camels. Choose a large tract of land (to be the lord of), and live yourself for as many autumns as you wish.

The Upanishatkaara is trying to show how, if all the wealth in the world is placed on one side of the balance, it still is no match for spiritual knowledge on the other.

Yama continues suggesting bigger and better temptations –

एतत्तुल्यं यदि मन्यसे वरं
वृणीष्व वित्तं चिरजीविकां च ।
महाभूमौ नचिकेतस्त्वमेधि
कामानां त्वा कामभाजं करोमि ॥ १।१।२४॥

O Nachiketaa! If you consider a boon to be equivalent (to the one you have asked for), take it – choose wealth and a very long life, be the lord of a huge realm. (Not only that) I will make you capable of enjoying all these desirables.

Very often we find in this world that in our youth we work hard to attain wealth to achieve our desires, but by the time we attain that wealth, we are no longer in a position to enjoy them, as we have become weak in body and mind by then. Yama draws our attention to this by telling us that it is vitally important that one has the capacity to enjoy the attractions of this world in order to derive pleasure from them.

Seeing Nachiketaa unflinching in his resolve, Yama brings out all the resources at his disposal, viz., the pleasures of Swarga Loka –

ये ये कामा दुर्लभा मर्त्यलोके
सर्वान् कामाँश्छन्दतः प्रार्थयस्व ।
इमा रामाः सरथाः सतूर्या
न हीदृशा लम्भनीया मनुष्यैः ।
आभिर्मत्प्रत्ताभिः परिचारयस्व
नचिकेतो मरणं मानुप्राक्षीः ॥१।१।२५॥

Ask freely for all the desires that are so difficult to fulfil in the Land of the Mortals (Martya-loka). (Look at) these beautiful women (Apsaraas of Swarga Loka), complete with chariots and musical instruments. The likes of these are not available to humans. Take them from me and make them serve you. But, O Nachiketaa, do not ask me about death.

The worldly person who takes up the spiritual path also sees all these temptations obstructing her way. Only on overcoming the desire for all these can the desire to attain God be fulfilled. In fact, God will most likely especially present all these temptations to test the will of the seeker, just as Yama – really God – is tempting Nachiketaa, the Soul, in this parable.

Nachiketaa remains steadfast in his resolve –

श्वोभावा मर्त्यस्य यदन्तकैतत्
सर्वेन्द्रियाणां जरयन्ति तेजः ।
अपि सर्वं जीवितमल्पमेव
तवैव वाहास्तव नृत्यगीते ॥१।१।२६॥

O Antaka (Yama)! (All these worldly pleasures that you have tried to charm me with are all) transient. (In fact,) they age the acuity of all the senses of mortals. Indeed, one's whole life is too short (to satiate one's desires)! (For this reason,) let these chariots and the songs and dances (of the Apsaraas) remain yours (because I do not care for them at all).

Yamaraaja is called Antaka as death brings everything to an end, or Anta.

Shwobhaava means Shwah = tomorrow and Bhaava = being, i.e., things that stay only till tomorrow, and will evaporate the day after. All worldly objects and the joys they bring have this nature – they are ephemeral, they degrade and then perish. We cannot even hold on to a drop of water, what to speak of bigger things! However, they leave behind a yearning for them. Thus, all worldly pleasures bring in sorrow through the backdoor.

Not only that, they age the senses. The more we consume, the more we need to consume, because the senses now require bigger doses to give the same pleasure. With each morsel, they lose their keenness.

And this ever-growing lust is like an ever-growing fire that does not die even on our deathbed. That is why we are so sorrowful when death approaches us – we always feel we have so much more to do and enjoy! The Yogi, on the other hand, is completely indifferent to life and death. That is why it is said that he has risen above both – they no longer generate fear or desire in him.

The author of the Upanishad, Rshi Katha, continues to teach us a lesson in renunciation through the medium of Nachiketaa –

न वित्तेन तर्पणीयो मनुष्यो
लप्स्यामहे वित्तमद्राक्ष्म चेत् त्वा ।
जीविष्यामो यावदीशिष्यसि त्वं
वरस्तु मे वरणीयः स एव ॥ १ । १ । २७ ॥

Man can never be satisfied with wealth. Now that we (i.e., I) have seen you, we will surely attain wealth (and) we will live as long as you are ruling. (So, what is the point in asking for such trinkets?!) For me, only that boon is worth choosing.

The sage king Manu, the first giver of law to mankind, too, has stressed the insatiability of the senses as follows:

न जातु कामः कामानामुपभोगेन शाम्यति ।
हविषा कृष्णवर्त्मेव भूय एवाभिवर्धते ॥ मनुस्मृतिः २।६९॥

i.e., undoubtedly, desires are not quenched by fulfilling them, just as fire only increases manifold by adding inflammable material to it. This is the first and biggest hurdle that the Yogi has to cross.

It is when the seeker gives up the whole world for God that God gratifies him with His presence and knowledge. The vision of God fulfils all the desires the seeker still nurtures or may do so in the future – nothing more remains to yearn for!

Nachiketaa further cites the futility of wishing for worldly wealth –

अजीर्यताममृतानामुपेत्य
जीर्यन् मर्त्यः क्वधःस्थः प्रजानन् ।
अभिध्यायन् वर्णरतिप्रमोदा-
नतिदीर्घे जीविते को रमेत ॥१।१।२८॥

Having come close to those who do not age and do not die (i.e., you), an aging mortal comes to know that he resides in a lesser, lower sphere. Knowing this and pondering over (the ephemerality of) the beauty and sexual pleasures (of partners), who will delight in an extra-long life?!

Somebody who has seen 'the colour of the grass on the other side' cannot possibly be satisfied by the pleasures of the world down under. The ecstasy of not aging or dying far outweighs the delights of mundane Material experiences. Nachiketaa says, 'I have seen you and understood life on this side. Trying to tempt me with the world down under is futile.'

While the spiritual seeker can never really see first-hand what life in the other world is like, he must believe in the promise that learned sages hold out, like Katha, the author of this Upanishad, that there is indeed such a place where one is free of old age, sorrow and death.

Kvadhahstha = ku (bad) + adhah (below) + stha (situated), i.e., one who is situated in the sorrowful nether world.

Nachiketaa rests his case by repeating his most potent argument –

यस्मिन्निदं विचिकित्सन्ति मृत्यो

यत्साम्पराये महति ब्रूहि नस्तत् ।

योऽयं वरो गूढमनुप्रविष्टो

नान्यं तस्मान्नचिकेता वृणीते ॥१।१।२९॥

O Death! In this grave matter of the other world (of whether someone survives death or not), in which (even the learned) have doubts, please preach that to me! Nachiketaa does not choose anything other than this boon that enters into a subtle realm (an extremely difficult subject).

It is with great difficulty that one finds a teacher who understands the other world, who is steeped in God, who has completely renounced this world. Most god-persons that we see today can be seen to be conducting worldly business, while being happy to be called God themselves. A person close to God will never abide such blasphemy, because he understands well the chasm that separates the Creator, Protector and Destroyer of this Universe vis-à-vis the individual Soul. The student who is lucky enough to find such a person should not give up the chance to learn from this master, whatever obstacles or temptations – of which there will be many – that may lie in this path.

The end of this section essentially marks the end of the story of Yama and Nachiketaa, though references are interspersed in the rest of the Upanishad, too. Henceforth the Upanishatkaara focuses on the teaching that he really wants to pass on.

SECTION II: THE TWO PATHS IN LIFE

This second section of the first chapter introduces the worldly-wise person to another path that is available which leads to a place not visible to the senses.

Rshi Katha introduces the subject in his simple but impactful way –

अन्यच्छ्रेयोऽन्यदुतैव प्रेयस्-

ते उभे नानार्थे पुरुषँ सिनीतः ।

तयोः श्रेय आददानस्य साधु

भवति हीयतेऽर्थाद्य उ प्रेयो वृणीते ॥१।२।१॥

(In this world) there is that which is worthy (Shreya) and then another that is pleasant (Preya). Both of them bind the Soul to different goals. Among the two, the one who picks Shreya chooses well; the one who selects Preya loses out on the real goal of life.

Shreya refers to that which leads towards salvation (Moksha), while Preya consists of worldly temptations. Yama had offered Preya to Nachiketaa, but he had steadfastly refused it. Thus, he was a fit candidate for the goal of salvation. Since Shreya and Preya do not go together, one has to be selected over the other. So, ancient sages often tested the commitment of the student to Shreya, as Yama did for Nachiketaa.

Human life is the only one where the option of Moksha is available. Moksha is so far removed from other animals and beings that they cannot even consider it. They are all stuck in Preya. For this reason, for the human being it is the ultimate goal – any other goal is just a waste of a human birth...

Even if we do not attain Moksha in this very birth, the recommended life cycle in the Indian system[12] is custom-made to

---

12 *Refer Introduction, points 11 and 12.*

ensure that we always head in that direction across births.

Yama elaborates further –

श्रेयश्च प्रेयश्च मनुष्यमेतस्‍-
तौ सम्परीत्य विविनक्ति धीरः ।
श्रेयो हि धीरोऽभि प्रेयसो वृणीते
प्रेयो मन्दो योगक्षेमाद् वृणीते ॥१।२।२॥

Both Shreya and Preya approach the human. The resolute ones (Dheera) ponder over the two deeply and separate one from the other. The Dheera, then, accepts the worthy one over the pleasant one, while the feeble-minded selects Preya to fulfil his worldly desires of accumulating worldly riches (Yoga) and protecting them from decay or destruction (Kshema).

The world surrounds us all, and its attractions attract all beings from the weakest to the strongest. Thus, not much deliberation is required to take up worldly activities to increase our comforts, our enjoyments and our delights. Towards this end, each person works in two directions – one towards accumulating wealth and the other towards protecting that which has been acquired. These two are called Yoga and Kshema, respectively. Yoga generically means union. So, persevering towards 'uniting with' (acquiring) wealth is the first activity. Kshema means taken care of. So, taking care of the acquired wealth is the next sphere of effort for a person. Of course, enjoyment of the wealth itself is implicit. These two are mentioned explicitly as they usually are unpleasant activities, but we spend most of our time doing them – far more than the enjoyment of the wealth itself!

Shreya, too, confronts us every day, in terms of the moral dilemmas that present themselves to us, the choice of performing benevolent deeds over selfish ones, the choice of pursuing knowledge over wealth, etc. The thinking person sees these choices and realises that the ethical choice does not necessarily yield any outcome in the short run, but only yields dividends in the long run. And those dividends far outweigh the short-term pleasures that we gain from Preya choices. He, thus, separates carefully one from the other and picks that which will ensure his future well-being.

Yama praises Nachiketaa for the choices he has made –

स त्वं प्रियान् प्रियरूपाँश्च कामा-
नभिध्यायन् नचिकेतोऽत्यस्राक्षीः ।
नैताँ सृङ्कां वित्तमयीमवाप्तो
यस्यां मज्जन्ति बहवो मनुष्याः ॥१।२।३॥

O Nachiketaa! (Among those Dheeras,) you considered all the desires that are pleasurable and are pleasant in appearance (that I placed before you), and then gave them up. You did not yield to these chains of wealth, in which sink many a human.

As we saw earlier, Nachiketaa put forth incisive arguments against the best pleasures of the world that Yama had offered. To begin with, most people do not have the mental capacity to think over these issues. Even when they do, they are unable to accept the results and continue sinking deeper and deeper into the mire that is this world with its myriad attractions. Rare are those who see through the trappings and are able to take action against them! Nachiketaa, for all his tender years, was one of those and Yama recognises that well.

Yama elaborates –

दूरमेते विपरीते विषूची
अविद्या या च विद्येति ज्ञाता ।
विद्याभीप्सिनं नचिकेतसं मन्ये
न त्वा कामा बहवोऽलोलुपन्त ॥१।२।४॥

These two (Shreya and Preya) are far from each other and in opposite directions. They are known as ignorance (Avidyaa, i.e., Preya) and knowledge (Vidyaa, i.e., Shreya). I believe that you, Nachiketaa, are desirous of Vidyaa. (That is why) the many desirable things (that I presented to you) were unable to tempt you.

Sometimes we feel that if we lead a righteous life, we will automatically attain Moksha. While this is an important first step in attaining Moksha, deliberate steps have to be taken towards Moksha itself in order to achieve it. This may be seen as obtaining a PhD: while kindergarten plays an important role in taking a student to the level of PhD, reaching the latter stage requires such a huge leap that kindergarten pales into insignificance. It is often a hard thing to understand that without renouncing the world, it is impossible to achieve the ultimate goal of human existence. Of course, renunciation itself is not possible if we did not lead a blameless life to begin with, but this is only a necessary condition, not a sufficient one. That is why Yama says that these two tracks are far apart and point in opposite directions.

Of these, the worldly pleasures require little knowledge. We may think that to become the CEO of a multinational requires a lot of knowledge and skill, but they pale in comparison to the knowledge and self-control required for spiritual endeavours. In fact, the former may well be called ignorance in contrast, i.e, Avidyaa! The strange thing is that people on the worldly track can stay completely oblivious to the spiritual one.

However, even those on the spiritual path can be misled and need to be cautious. Yama now describes such people in a famous verse –

अविद्यायामन्तरे वर्तमानाः

स्वयं धीराः पण्डितम्मन्यमानाः ।

दन्द्रम्यमाणाः परियन्ति मूढा

अन्धेनैव नीयमाना यथान्धाः ॥ १।२।५॥[13]

---

13 *This verse is also found in Mundakopanishad (1/2/8).*

There are those who are entrenched in Avidyaa, (but who) believe that they are sagacious (Dheeras) and learned ones (Panditas). Those fools go hither and thither, committing sins everywhere, just as blind persons who are led by another blind man (go about knocking into every other obstacle and falling into every other pit).

This famous verse describes eloquently the state of those who do not know – and do not know that they do not know! In fact, they are quite sure that they know it all and there is nothing more to be known. Led by their false beliefs, they keep committing sins and never pause to look inwards.

The body and the senses it is endowed with are so powerful that it is very difficult to believe that there is another world inside. It is easy to develop lust and run after the objects of the senses. And, of course, there is very little proof of that other world, except for the words of those who have seen it! The cost of this delusion is the sorrow that befalls worldly pursuits. Yama puts it poetically –

न साम्परायः प्रतिभाति बालं

प्रमाद्यन्तं वित्तमोहेन मूढम् ।

अयं लोको नास्ति पर इति मानी

पुनः पुनर्वशमापद्यते मे ॥१।२।६॥

In a childlike person who is deluded by the lust for worldly riches and, shying away (from the proper path), deep thought (of that other inner world) does not arise. He believes that this (visible expanse) is the (only) world and none other exists. Because of this, he comes into my clutches again and again (i.e., remains entrapped in the Cycle of Life and Death).

Foolish persons are simple-minded like children – they need their wishes to be fulfilled immediately. Long-term considerations do not appeal to them. We can understand this with the analogy of a lottery that is won by a foolish person vis-à-vis that won by a wise person. The fool and his money are soon parted, while the intelligent person saves it for the future and makes it grow. Similarly, the spiritually-challenged do not have the intellect or the patience to analyse their actions and their consequences. Even if they are capable of such introspection, they somehow come to the conclusion that this is the only life, and there could be no other. So, an all-out effort must be made to fulfil all one's desires, and the means become subservient to the end. We see most of the world caught in this trap, for the fact that there is a Soul that survives death, and continues to bear the consequences of the actions done today in later lives, is not obvious at all. Even when their conscience is active, they may be unable to accept another world where there is only a Soul, unencumbered by a body, enjoying an existence so devoid of sorrow that it can hardly be described.

The one who seeks out a spiritual path is rare indeed!

If the person who sets out on a spiritual journey is rare, how much rarer must be the one who can show him the way –

श्रवणायापि बहुभिर्यो न लभ्यः

शृण्वन्तोऽपि बहवो यं न विद्युः ।

आश्चर्यो वक्ता कुशलोऽस्य लब्धा-

श्र्यो ज्ञाता कुशलानुशिष्टः ॥ १।२।७॥

Many do not even hear of it (the Soul). Even on hearing, many do not understand it. The one who describes it is amazing; the one who understands it is proficient. The one who knows about it is remarkable; the one who follows his teaching is skilful.

This statement holds good even today. How many have heard of the eternal Soul? How many bother about it even when they do hear? Even among those who profess to know about it, there are few who can explain it to another. And for the student to understand it, like Nachiketaa, she should have done enough penance already before learning from the master.

Here, one may wonder what is so great about learning about the Soul. Particularly in India, one is exposed to the concept of a Soul from the very beginning of one's life and has no problem in accepting this fact. However, do we really understand this Soul? What traits belong to the body and what traits are the Soul's alone? When you reflect deeply on the subject, you realise how little you really know about the individual Soul…

Yama puts this fact in verse –

न नरेणावरेण प्रोक्त एष

सुविज्ञेयो बहुधा चिन्त्यमानः ।

अनन्यप्रोक्ते गतिरत्र नास्ति

अणीयान् ह्यतर्क्यमणुप्रमाणात् ॥१।२।८॥

When this truth is told by a lesser human, it is not properly understood even after putting in much thought. When told by an ordinary person, there is no understanding (by the listener, because) the Soul is subtler than an atom and is beyond reasoning.

Today, we have no difficulty in accepting spiritual teachings based on blind faith, with no reasoning involved, not even any reality check! However, for a true seeker, it is important to know the truth and nothing but the truth. For this, she has to herself experience that which is being told. Only the most remarkable teacher can teach a student where to look for the Soul and how to find it in the depths of one's being.

Today's preachers may induce a drug-like ecstasy, but does that create a lasting righteousness, a lasting renunciation, a lasting bliss in the follower? Momentary ecstasy is provided by many things – a lover's kiss, divine music, a difficult hurdle crossed, even drugs. How, then, can we distinguish between what is real and what is fake?

Yama explains further –

नैषा तर्केण मतिरापनेया

प्रोक्तान्येनैव सुज्ञानाय प्रेष्ठ ।

यां त्वमापः सत्यधृतिर्बतासि

त्वाद्दङ्नो भूयान् नचिकेतः प्रष्टा ॥१।२।९॥

O beloved (Nachiketaa)! This (knowledge) that you have obtained is not available through reasoning. It can only be properly understood when told by another (who has experienced it personally). You are indeed one of true steadfastness. May we find more inquirers like you!

Yama is again overcome with affection for Nachiketaa, a student like none other he has met – one who is steadfast in his quest and not swayed from his goal. Indeed, he talks to him as if Nachiketaa has already acquired the wisdom he is yet to impart, for in his mind, there is no doubt that Nachiketaa shall acquire it!

The fact that the spirit cannot be gauged by reason alone is repeated many more times in this Upanishad, and in other ancient Indian texts as well. It is, in fact, for this reason that scientists still doubt its existence. It is like meeting somebody who has been on the moon – we can never comprehend what walking on the moon is like unless we hear it from 'the horse's mouth'. The same is true in spirituality – we will continue to live our lives as if we will last only as long as the body, until we meet someone who has 'seen' the Soul.

Yama describes his own secret formula for attaining the Soul –

जानाम्यहँ शेवधिरित्यनित्यं

न ह्यध्रुवैः प्राप्यते हि ध्रुवं तत् ।

ततो मया नाचिकेतश्चितोऽग्नि-

रनित्यैर्द्रव्यैः प्राप्तवानस्मि नित्यम् ॥१।२।१०॥

I know that wealth is but transient. With transient wealth, that eternal (Soul) cannot be obtained. That is why the Naachiketa Agni (Yajna) was performed (devised) by me. With transient substances (used in the Yajna), I attained the eternal (Soul).

It is difficult to accept this statement of the performance of a Yajna yielding the desired goal of a spiritual seeker. Yama himself had described that Yajna to attain tremendous happiness in the form of Swarga. The next verse indicates that any number of Yajnas cannot lead one to the Soul. Some commentators have taken the Yajna here to refer to meditation. However, since the Naachiketa Agni is clearly specified as a fire-sacrifice in the previous chapter, it is difficult to ascribe another meaning to it here. And yet, later statements, too, corroborate the meaning of Samaadhi (see verse 1|3|2, for example). The transient substances mentioned here, then, are the elements that make up the body, and more so the mind. Yama confirms that the body, too, is indispensable in the search for the Divine.

Yama again praises Nachiketaa for his steadfastness –

कामस्याप्तिं जगतः प्रतिष्ठां

क्रतोरनन्त्यमभयस्य पारम् ।

स्तोममहदुरुगायं प्रतिष्ठां

दृष्ट्वा धृत्या धीरो नचिकेतोऽत्यस्राक्षीः ॥१।२।११॥

O Nachiketaa! Seeing the (temptations I offered for) fulfilment of desires, fame in this world, infinite (great) auspiciousness from Yajnas, the end of fear, great praise and status that is praised by many, you considered them and gave them up. (Therefore, I think that) you are extremely intelligent.

The various temptations that Yama presented to Nachiketaa are generally divided into three –

1) Desire for family and progeny (Putraishanaa)

2) Desire for wealth and comforts (Vittaishanaa)

3) Desire for power and status, as also the attainment of Swarga Loka through Yajnas, generosity to others, etc. (Lokaishanaa).

These succinctly categorise all our worldly desires.

Yama praises Nachiketaa saying that normal people would have fallen for one or the other of these and given up the quest for the Ultimate, but you stayed the course.

Yama moves to the teaching proper –

तं दुर्दर्शं गूढमनुप्रविष्टं

गुहाहितं गह्वरेष्ठं पुराणम् ।

अध्यात्मयोगाधिगमेन देवं

मत्वा धीरो हर्षशोकौ जहाति ॥१।२।१२॥

That which is difficult to attain through the senses, is hidden, enters the body after its creation and after the Soul, is situated in the 'cave' of the mind, in the most difficult-to-reach places and is ancient (i.e., eternal) – that Divine Being is to be attained by performing Adhyaatma-yoga. Knowing this being, the steadfast seeker loses all happiness and sorrow.

While the Lord is omnipresent and one does not have to go anywhere to find Him, He is to be found in a specific place in the body, or more specifically, the brain (often called the 'heart' in spiritual texts). This is often referred to as the 'Guhaa' or cave in the Vedas and spiritual texts. When the seeker meditates deeply (called Samaadhi), she feels as if she has entered a cave where the senses stop sending any signals to interrupt the Soul. The meditator then finds first one's own self and then, as if hidden behind it, the Lord. This is called 'Adhyaatma-yoga', the finding of the Soul. Patanjali explains the steps to achieve this in his immortal text *Yogadarshanam*. The steep and arduous path to that enlightenment requires extreme perseverance and self-control. That is why the seeker has to be a Dheera!

The moment the separate existence of the Soul is experienced first-hand, all attachment to the body is shed instantly, and along with it all happiness and sorrow dependent on the body.

Preachers sometimes say that the vision of God removes all the sorrow and then only bliss, or unadulterated happiness, remains. But all ancient spiritual texts tell us that both sorrow and happiness are lost then – not only sorrow. This is because happiness of a worldly nature, i.e., related to the body and the senses, is sorrow too. Not only does it make us crave for worldly pleasures, but it hooks us to the body and makes us give up our ultimate quest (more about this in the next section).

Yama continues –

एतच्छुत्वा सम्परिगृह्य मर्त्यः

प्रवृह्य धर्म्यमणुमेतमाप्य ।

स मोदते मोदनीयँ हि लब्ध्वा

विवृतँ सद्म नचिकेतसं मन्ये ॥१।२।१३॥

When a mortal (human being) hears about This (Brahma) and grasps It properly, contemplates on It, he attains that infinitesimal Being that is the Source of Dharma. Attaining the Blissful, he also becomes blissful. I believe that the doors of that abode are wide open for Nachiketaa.

Yama outlines the four steps to enlightenment in a nutshell. These are well known as Shravan-chatushtaya in Shaastras. He says that, first, one has to hear (or read) about these concepts (Shravana), as they are not ones that come to us naturally. And if one does not know what one is looking for, one is unlikely to ever find it. So, gaining knowledge about the spirit world is Step 1.

In Step 2, one has to examine the new learning from all angles (Manana), ask all kinds of questions, have all kinds of doubts, which one should resolve oneself by further thought, studies or by approaching a master. Any number of iterations of this process are acceptable.

In Step 3, one internalises the now well-understood and accepted

information (Nididhyaasana) and makes it one's own. Every part of it should be crystal clear and installed in one's memory.

In Step 4, the seeker should contemplate over those ideas and meditate in the recesses of his mind. The object of his contemplations then presents itself directly (Sakshaatkaara). This attainment (Praapti) is what opens the doors to the spirit world that the seeker may enter at will.

God is called 'Dharmya' as He is the source and the embodiment of all the natural laws, or Dharma, that rule this Universe. No such law can be broken because He is there to ensure that it is rigidly followed. Righteousness is also called Dharma. This is because the right way of living is to ensure that one lives according to the laws of the Universe. Living this way, one attains happiness; if not, grief. This may be likened to stroking wild grass – when it is stroked in the direction of its bristles, it is smooth; if stroked the opposite way, the bristles can even cut the skin!

God is also the subtlest thing (Anu) in the Universe; Matter or Prakrti is the grossest and the Soul is somewhere in between. Thus, for the Soul to reach God, it literally has to look inside itself. This is the reason why the term 'Anupravishta' was used in the previous verse, meaning 'situated later' – not physically, but in terms of where It is to be found.

Yama has seen that Nachiketaa has satisfied the first requirement of enlightenment, i.e., overcoming sensory desires. He has also seen his sharp intellect by which he quickly learnt about the Naachiketa Agni. So, Yama has no doubt that he will accomplish Steps 2 and 3 without a hitch. It is sometimes professed that intelligence is not a factor in achieving God, but this is far from the truth. Without a very sharp intellect and phenomenal memory, it is not possible to attain spiritual heights. That is why education of the mind and Yogaasanas for the body have been such a basic requirement in the Indian system of education. For those not familiar with the practice, Yogaasanas can improve your IQ too!

Getting a little embarrassed by the praise that Yama is heaping on him, Nachiketaa stops his flow with a question –

अन्यत्र धर्मादन्यत्राधर्मादन्यत्रास्मात् कृताकृतात् ।
अन्यत्र भूताच्च भव्याच्च यत् तत् पश्यसि तद्वद ॥१।२।१४॥

That which is different from righteousness (Dharma) and from unrighteousness (Adharma), different from this effect (this Universe/ Brahmaanda) and its cause (primordial Matter/Prakrti),[14] different from the past, the present and the future – that which you see (so clearly), please tell me about it.

Nachiketaa once again proves his quick grasp of all that is being taught to him. Yama has just mentioned that all Dharma originates from a Source. Being a Source, It could not be the substance too. Thus, that object had to be different from Dharma and from Adharma (where Adharma is not the absence of Dharma, but the presence of its opposite). Also, if It is extremely subtle, it could not be the Universe; neither could It be the Material cause of the Universe, as Its properties are entirely different from it.[15] Since Time is also an effect of Matter, It has to be different from Time as well.

In this way, Nachiketaa proves himself to be a fitting student for the teaching that is to be imparted, which is so deep that it is often classified as 'Rahasya' or mystery.

Yama senses the urgency in Nachiketaa's request and approaches the subject directly –

सर्वे वेदा यत् पदमामनन्ति
तपाँसि सर्वाणि च यद्वदन्ति ।
यदिच्छन्तो ब्रह्मचर्यं चरन्ति
तत् ते पदँ सङ्ग्रहेण ब्रवीम्योमित्येतत् ॥१।२।१५॥

---

14 See Introduction, points 1-3.
15 See Introduction, point 1.

That goal which the Vedas repeatedly declare, that which is the goal of all austerities, desirous of which (Yogis) perform chastity, that goal I tell you in brief – it is Om.

Om is the eternal and personal name of Paramaatmaa that is unique to Him. In Paanini's work, the Dhaatupaatha, several meanings are listed for each Sanskrit verb root. In that work, 21 meanings are ascribed to the root 'Ava' from which the word 'Om' originates – the largest number ascribed to any root, and each of those 21 meanings applies to God! Many other Upanishads talk about the various meanings of each syllable that 'Om' is composed of – a, u, m – and the importance of meditating upon each syllable separately, as well as the conjoined syllable, 'Om'.

Realisation of the Lord is the supreme goal of this human life. Therefore, it is the primary purpose of the Vedas. It is, too, the reason that all the seekers go through enormous self-deprivation and austerities.

The Upanishatkaara elaborates –

एतत्ध्येवाक्षरं ब्रह्म एतत्ध्येवाक्षरं परम् ।
एतत्ध्येवाक्षरं ज्ञात्वा यो यदिच्छति तस्य तत् ॥१।२।१६॥

This syllable (Om, as mentioned in the previous verse) alone is Brahma. It alone is the greatest. Knowing this syllable, whatever one desires, it becomes his.

Om is the most powerful syllable to attain Brahma. It is Brahma's personal name for a reason. It encompasses so many qualities of Brahma, that it almost represents Brahma completely. And once Brahma is known, Its various qualities are understood, all that one desires, or can desire, is attained – this is the promise of not only this Upanishad but all Vaidika texts. The fact is that once Brahma is attained, the seeker experiences an ecstasy that one might experience when all one's desires are met simultaneously – and then some!

Further –

एतदालम्बनँ श्रेष्ठमेतदालम्बनं परम् ।
एतदालम्बनं ज्ञात्वा ब्रह्मलोके महीयते ॥१।२।१७॥

This syllable (Om) is the best support, the greatest support (for achieving Brahma). Knowing this support, (the Yoginee) becomes great in the abode of Brahma.

Chanting Om (Japa), contemplating on its various meanings, focuses the mind in meditation and takes one close to Brahma quickly. Patanjali, in his Yogadarshanam, has prescribed the Japa of Om for focusing the mind.[16] Most other Upanishads and allied texts have sung paeans of this syllable, saying that the word and what it stands for are almost one. One can oneself experience the meditative quality of this syllable. It seems to directly elevate one to cosmic heights![17]

Many Mantras are prevalent today for performing meditation, but this is the best. In fact, it would not be an exaggeration to say that without this syllable, it is impossible for the seeker to discover the Lord.

Having explained briefly the nature of Brahma, Yama now speaks of the eternal individual Soul –

न जायते म्रियते वा विपश्चिन्-
नायं कुतश्चिन्न बभूव कश्चित् ।
अजो नित्यः शाश्वतोऽयं पुराणो
न हन्यते हन्यमाने शरीरे ॥१।२।१८॥[18]

---

16 *तस्य वाचकः प्रणवः ॥ तज्जपस्तदर्थभावनम् ॥योगदर्शनम् १।२७-८॥*

17 *It is so significant that other faiths also seem to have adopted it, though its importance is not well understood by them. Christianity's 'Amen', Islam's 'Aameen', etc., seem to be derived from 'Om', which itself is composed of* अव + मन्. *In the above two examples, the last 'n' has been retained, while it elides in the formation of* ओम्.

18 *In the Bhagawad-geetaa, the verse appears as follows –* न जायते म्रियते वा कदाचिन्नायं भूत्वा भविता वा न भूयः । अजो नित्यः *शाश्वतोऽयं पुराणो न हन्यते हन्यमाने शरीरे ॥२।२०॥ - where the meaning is "The Soul is never born, nor does it ever die; nor does it cease to exist again after having existed, i.e., it is not as if it has no beginning but does have an end. (Rest as above.)"*

The Soul that is the observer and the knower (in this Material body) is not born, nor does it die; it has not come from anywhere and nor does it become anyone/anything. It is unborn, unchanging, without an end or a beginning. It is not killed when the body is destroyed.

'Vipashchit' means 'an observer who sees more than usual'. It thus connotes a wise person who sees more than meets the eye, just like the English word 'seer'. However, here the word refers to the Soul, in general, because the Soul collects the inputs from all the senses and, with the help of the mind and the intellect, collates it into a single meaningful reality.

The fact that the Soul does not arise from anywhere, and nor does it give rise to anything implies that it is neither an effect of anything, nor a cause for something. There is a belief that the Soul is born out of Brahma and dissolves back into It, i.e., it is an effect of Brahma; but as in this verse, and in many verses of other Upanishads, this view is not supported by ancient texts. The Soul is unborn, unchanging and unending. The good and bad attributes it seems to have are born out of the body and end with it. As Patanjali says in *Yogadarshanam* – द्रष्टा दृशिमात्रः शुद्धोऽपि प्रत्ययानुपश्यः (२।२०) – the seer (Soul) is only a witness and remains pure (untouched by Matter) while perceiving from its senses.

Most human civilisations (that did not come into contact with the teaching of the Vedas) intuitively realised that the Soul somehow survives the body, but they were not able to figure out how and why. That is why we have the Egyptians, Incas and others embalming the body and taking care of it in the belief that the Soul will return to it one day. Many present day religions continue with this belief in some form or the other. Reincarnation is a difficult concept for humans to figure out by themselves – God has to explain it to Man in the form of the Vedas!

The eternity of the Soul is further emphasised –

हन्ता चेन्मन्यते हन्तुँ हतश्चेन्मन्यते हतम् ।
उभौ तौ न विजानीतो नायं हन्ति न हन्यते ॥१।२।१९॥[19]

If a killer thinks he is capable of killing, and the one being killed thinks he has been killed, then neither of them know that this (Soul) neither kills, nor is it killed.

This famous verse describes the difficulty in accepting the immortality of the Soul. Since we see only the external body, and the Soul is invisible to us, we sometimes overlook its reality. But that is only our delusion!

Shifting focus to the Supreme, the seer says –

अणोरणीयान् महतो महीया-
नात्मास्य जन्तोर्निहितो गुहायाम् ।
तमक्रतुः पश्यति वीतशोको
धातुप्रसादान् महिमानमात्मनः ॥१।२।२०॥

Being subtler than the subtlest, and larger than the largest, (the Supreme) is the soul of the living being and is situated in the cave (of its Soul). A non-doer and one who has gone beyond sorrow sees the greatness of that (Supreme) Soul by the grace of the Bearer (the Supreme Himself).

The Lord is the subtlest of the three entities (Paramaatmaa, Jeevaatmaa and Prakrti[20]) that inhabit this Universe. At the same time, it is the largest of the three and extends beyond the Universe. Why then is it referred to as being situated inside the individual Soul? Because that is where the seeker has to seek him – not in the temple, not in the Teertha (sacred water-bodies that are supposed to wash away one's sins), not in the mountains, not in the trees, not

---

19 In the Bhagawad-geetaa, the verse appears as follows – य एनं वेत्ति हन्तारं यश्चैनं मन्यते हतम् । उभौ तौ न विजानीतो नायं हन्ति न हन्यते ॥२।१९॥ - where the different first line means: The one who believes this (Soul) to be the killer and the one who believes this (Soul) to have been killed...
20 See Introduction, point 1.

116

in the Sun, but in oneself, in the recesses of one's Soul. Many may feel at peace in front of a statue, many others in the lap of Nature, but the true seeker has to find the true God, and is not satisfied with symbols, just like an orphan seeking her parents cannot be satisfied with a photograph of a couple.

The beauty of this search is that God alone will reveal Himself when He finds an opportune moment, when He feels the seeker has searched enough, has renounced enough, has suffered enough. Having seen the Lord in her own Soul, the seeker becomes a non-doer – she realises that actually all action is Matter acting on Matter; the Soul can will the body but actually it is the body that performs all the actions with the Soul always untouched by the action or its consequence. This is a very subtle point and should be pondered over deeply. Many believe that it is possible to do selfless Karma without seeing one's true nature, but this is not so. Only when one sees one's true nature does s/he realise that the Soul is always untouched by Matter; it only mistakenly believes itself to be Matter and suffers the consequences of that misunderstanding. Once this enlightenment occurs, the Soul sheds all sorrow and roams unfettered and untouched.[21]

The sage further describes Brahma and His enigmatic nature –

आसीनो दूरं व्रजति शयानो याति सर्वतः ।
कस्तं मदामदं देवं मदन्यो ज्ञातुमर्हति ॥१।२।२१॥

While being seated, (the Divine) roams far. While lying down, He travels everywhere. Who can know that blissful (Mada) and equanimous (Amada) Divine other than me?!

Brahma is full of contradictions, because He is not made up of Prakrti, whose properties alone we comprehend. One has to transcend the usual, the mundane, to see and understand this

---

21 *Akratu (non-doer) and Veetashoka (one beyond grief) are thus the effect of the true vision attained by the seer, and not the cause of it, as is often interpreted in the verse.*

amazing Being. He is at rest and yet moving, because He is present everywhere and so cannot move, yet seems to travel to the farthest points of the Universe along with all the objects that move inside it. He is full of bliss and yet devoid of the joy or lust created by the enjoyment of worldly pleasures.

The seer exults that so strange is this Being that surely someone has to have travelled this long and arduous road like me to see Him, and I see no such person around me!

Continuing in ecstasy, the sage says –

अशरीरँ शरीरेष्वनवस्थेष्ववस्थितम् ।
महान्तं विभुमात्मानं मत्वा धीरो न शोचति ॥१।२।२२॥

Knowing that great, all-pervasive Soul (Brahma) that is without a body and unchanging inside the transient bodies (of living beings), the steadfast seeker does not grieve.

The Lord resides inside all, yet is untouched by the properties of what He occupies. The bodies of living things are occupied by the individual Soul, and that too remains untouched by the properties of the body. Being subtler, the Lord occupies even these Souls and remains unaffected by them. While the Soul has control over its body, the Lord is only an observer inside. Therefore, He is truly Ashareeree (without a body), while the Soul is Shareeree (with a body). Therefore, while the Soul has to leave its residence when the body dies, the Lord does not have to undergo even that much uprooting. Pervading all Space and Time, He is the same everywhere.

The seer explains how difficult it is to attain that Supreme –

नायमात्मा प्रवचनेन लभ्यो
न मेधया न बहुना श्रुतेन ।
यमेवैष वृणुते तेन लभ्यस्-
तस्यैष आत्मा विवृणुते तनूँ स्वाम् ॥१।२।२३॥

That (Param-)Aatmaa cannot be attained by sermonising, nor through the intellect, nor by listening (to a lot of spiritual discourses). (In fact,) the one whom He selects, that person alone attains Him, and to that Soul this (Great) Soul reveals His true 'body' (i.e., form).

Having just said above that the Supreme has no form, in this verse the seer says 'Swaam Tanoom' – His body or form. These kinds of contradictions arise because words start falling short in describing God. Experiencing Him goes beyond the senses; only the Soul itself can 'see' Him. But our language is centred on the experiences of our body and our senses. As we probe deeper, words start becoming insufficient…

Similarly, by the seer's admonition that all that he has recommended so far is actually futile, one should not think that it is completely so. It is like doing PhD after getting all the necessary degrees up to that stage – all those degrees are necessary, but far from sufficient to cross the final chasm. In the search for Brahma, Brahma Himself determines who has become worthy to find Him and then reveals Himself in all His glory!

The seer continues to describe for whom the Supreme is not reachable –

नाविरतो दुश्चरितान्नाशान्तो नासमाहितः ।

नाशान्तमानसो वापि प्रज्ञानेनैनमाप्नुयात् ॥१।२।२४॥

The one who does not abstain from wrong deeds, is restless, has not attained the focus of mind required for deep meditation (Samaadhi), is anxious and troubled inside, that person cannot attain Him even through deep spiritual knowledge.

While gaining knowledge by listening and studying, by the intellect and by teaching yield proximity to God, this verse tells us that deep meditation is the final step to 'see' the Divine. However, those who have not distanced themselves from the world and are therefore restless and nervous, for them even the contemplation of the Lord is out of the question. For those who have gained some peace internally, practising focusing the mind is the next step towards salvation.

Today, gurus are ready to put large crowds into a meditative trance, with no concern as to their moral rectitude. While the power of suggestion of their words may give us some momentary peace, to attain eternal peace, all austerities, self-study, moral corrections, contemplation and quiet meditation are required – this is what the verse declares in no uncertain terms.

'Prajnaa' is a word that indicates knowledge derived through spiritual contemplation. As the Soul purifies itself, its inherent knowledge, covered by the ignorance generated by the body, is slowly but surely exposed. This is Prajnaa.

Finally, the seer sets the boundary for even the spiritually advanced seeker –

यस्य ब्रह्म च क्षत्रं च उभे भवत ओदनः ।
मृत्युर्यस्योपसेचनं क इत्था वेद यत्र सः ॥१।२।२५॥

For Whom the power of knowledge and that of physical strength are both but food and Death is but the curry (that goes with it), who knows where and how He is?!

The verse implies that even when the Soul does come to see the Divine, by His ultimate grace, then, too, who can divine completely the One who is everywhere and everything?! He embodies all knowledge and all action in this Universe. He consumes all beings, as it were, at the end of the Universal Cycle,[22] even destroying Death in the process. When we ourselves are not there at some place, at that time and in that place, how can we know Him? Thus, the verse sets out the limits to the reach of the Soul. To think that the Soul can ever gain full knowledge of Him, or become Him, is foolish!

---

22 See Introduction, point 3

120

With this final sermon on how and to what extent the Lord can be realised, the chapter draws to a close.

SECTION III: FINDING THE ULTIMATE

This third section of the first chapter deals almost exclusively with the relationship between the three entities that make up this world, in particular Brahma and the Jeevaatmaa.

The sage describes the structure of the body vis-à-vis the Soul and God –

ऋतं पिबन्तौ सुकृतस्य लोके

गुहां प्रविष्टौ परमे परार्धे ।

छायातपौ ब्रह्मविदो वदन्ति

पञ्चाग्रयो ये च त्रिणाचिकेताः ॥ १।३।१ ॥

Bound by the laws of Nature, in the abode of good deeds (the human body), the two (Brahma and the Jeevaatmaa) are situated in the ultimate and penultimate regions of the cave (of the mind), like shadow and light – this is what the knowers of Brahma and those who have performed the Panch Mahayajnas[23] faithfully, and those who have performed the Naachiketa Yajna thrice, say.

The sage has said many things in this small verse! Firstly, it is worth noting that the body itself is called 'Loka', as we had said in verse 1|1|3. The human body is special, because it is the only one in which we can hope to meet our Maker. This implies that it is attained with great effort, a surfeit of good deeds.

'Drinking truth' as some commentators have said of 'Rtam Pibantau' makes no sense whatsoever, as the Jeevaatmaa is covered with untruth or ignorance, the shackles of which it still has to

---

23 *See Introduction, point 12.*

break asunder. 'Rta' is actually a word very often used to describe the natural order of the Universe. This is the Rta that binds the Jeevaatmaa and even God to the extent that He, too, has to follow the Laws of Creation that He Himself has formulated.

The word 'Pravishtau' means 'entered'. The Soul enters the body and God follows, as it were, along with it. Where do they enter? In the cave of the mind (as explained in verse 1|2|12), with God taking up a position interior to the Soul, as He is subtler.

Here, the Soul is covered with ignorance. Therefore, it is like the dark shadow. God, on the other hand, remains radiant like sunlight. The allegory of darkness for ignorance and light for knowledge is a common one in Indian scriptures.

The Grhasthees and Vaanaprasthees perform the Panch Mahayajnas.[24] The verse indicates that even they can obtain enlightenment, albeit limited, if they perform their duties faithfully. Those who are alert about their duties automatically purify themselves. This opens the windows, if not the doors, of God's abode for them.

Only when we know how to search for the Supreme can we modify our actions accordingly. Only when we know where to look for Him can we look in the right place. This verse indicates some of both these parameters.

Yama again waxes eloquent about the Naachiketa Agni –

यः सेतुरीजानानामक्षरं ब्रह्म यत् परम् ।
अभयं तितीर्षतां पारं नाचिकेतँ शकेमहि ॥१।३।२॥

The One who is a bridge for those who perform Yajnas (i.e., good deeds), that which is indivisible (Akshara), huge (Brahma), ultimate (Para), fearless (Abhaya) and the other shore (Paara) for those swimming (in the sorrows of this world), that Naachiketa (Yajna) may

---

24 See Introduction, point 11 and 12.

we be capable of performing!

From the words used by Rshi Katha – Akshara, Brahma, Para, Abhaya, Paara – it is clear that the goal of the Naachiketa Yajna is the Supreme itself. It then follows that the Naachiketa Yajna itself is not a fire-sacrifice per se, but represents the highest level of meditation. The procedure that Yama had described in the first chapter, including the bricks and how they were to be placed (verse 1|1|15), actually referred to the method of performing the meditation, because it is only through meditation that we enter 'the cave of the mind' and see the two – the Soul and Brahma – 'drinking Rta' inside!

In this verse, too, the word 'Yajna' actually refers to all the good deeds, austerities and meditation that are performed by mortals to attain the Immortal. Of these, the Naachiketa meditation is the most superior and acts as a bridge over the troubled waters of this world to transport the seeker directly to her goal – Brahma and Moksha.

To further explain the three entities that occupy this body, in the next two verses, the sage details a metaphor from the Vedas[25] that is also found in the *Bhagawad-geetaa*. Hence, we take up the two verses together –

आत्मानँ रथिनं विद्धि शरीरँ रथमेव तु ।
बुद्धिं तु सारथिं विद्धि मनः प्रग्रहमेव च ॥ २।३।३॥

Know yourself (i.e., the Soul) to be the owner of the chariot that is the body. Know the intellect to be the charioteer and the mind to be the reins.

इन्द्रियाणि हयानाहुर्विषयाँस्तेषु गोचरान् ।
आत्मेन्द्रियमनोयुक्तं भोक्तेत्याहुर्मनीषिणः ॥ २।३।४॥

---

25 सुषारथिरश्वानिव यन्मनुष्यान् नेनीयतेऽभीशुभिर्वाजिन इव ... ॥यजुर्वेदः ३४।६॥ - The mind is like an able charioteer that leads human beings with great alacrity (hither and thither), just as well-trained steed are controlled with reins.

The senses are the horses (of this chariot), and sense-objects are the roads on which they wander. The thinkers call the Soul that is united with the senses and the mind (including the intellect) as the consumer.

In two short verses, the body-mind-Soul complex is laid bare! In this popular metaphor of the chariot, the body forms the chariot that is driven by horses that represent the senses. As we are all aware in our daily lives, most of our waking hours are spent in appeasing the senses – eating, drinking, entertaining, etc. All that we consume through our senses are the sense-objects. So, these latter form the road on which the senses traverse. 'Gochara', the word used for the road, is an apt term indeed, for it literally means 'where the cows walk', but the beauty is that the word 'Go' also refers to the senses. So, the word also means 'where the senses wander'!

These horses are unruly but they can be controlled – by means of the mind. God has given us a powerful device in the form of the mind that can perform the daily miracles that we so take for granted that we do not even notice them. For example, we can focus our attention exclusively on this book that we are reading and not allow the music we are hearing from the ears to disturb us. Yet, the mind continues to listen – it has just decided that this information is too harmless or unimportant to disturb the attention with. So, it filters it out. However, if a bomb were to explode in the neighbourhood, the mind would quickly pass on that information to the intellect and thence to the Soul, and initiate panic reactions within the body. Today, research is revealing the almost limitless power that the mind wields over the rest of the body – even healing the body when willed to do so by the Soul.

The intellect (Buddhi) is more subtle than the mind and acts as the charioteer that conveys the wishes of the owner to the chariot. While the mind is the executor, the intellect is the commander and interlocutor. When we expressly desire something, we send a message to the intellect. The Buddhi pads it up with all the stored information that is necessary for the execution of the command. It hands this over to the mind. The mind has all the information on what and how to make parts of the body react. It translates the command from the Buddhi into these motor messages. The Buddhi also makes sense of the sensory messages handed over by the Mana. In the example above, it is the Buddhi that comprehends what we are reading. It transmits this understanding to the Soul. The Soul remains mostly unaware of all this processing, just as the chariot-owner is unaware of the tugs on the reins.

When the Soul is connected to this paraphernalia, it responds to the sensory stimuli. It is then the 'consumer' of those signals from the Material World. When it is detached, it comes into its own. The objective of all spiritual treatises is to help you achieve that state.

The sage takes the metaphor further –

यस्त्वविज्ञानवान् भवत्ययुक्तेन मनसा सदा ।
तस्येन्द्रियाण्यवश्यानि दुष्टाश्वा इव सारथेः ॥१।३।५॥

The one who is incapable of discrimination and whose mind is always unfocused, that person's senses become out of control, just as the horses of a (careless) charioteer run wild and are out of his control.

Now, there are two pulls on this chariot – the owner may have a desire to go to point A, but the horses may be in the mood for straying into the meadow nearby. If the owner is not firm, the charioteer will also take it easy and the horses will become more and more uncontrolled. This is the situation that is to be avoided, and most spiritual texts teach us the importance and the ways and means of achieving this control over the intellect, mind and body. In this way, this metaphor really helps us to understand our relationship with our gross and subtle bodies[26] most aptly.

The senses of the body are always waiting to run amuck. The Soul has to always stay alert and rein them in. To do this, it has to first acquire the right knowledge, which tells it first and foremost that the senses need to be reined in. There continue to be many

____

26 See Introduction, Chart 1.

beliefs and social norms that promote continuous gratification of the senses. A higher calling is understood by but a few! The ones who do learn about this higher goal have to learn to train their mind and, through it, the senses, to turn the chariot towards that goal – something that is not quite appreciated by the senses as they start feeling deprived! With continuous practice, the mind and the senses do start behaving exactly as we wish, as the next verse elaborates –

यस्तु विज्ञानवान् भवति युक्तेन मनसा सदा ।
तस्येन्द्रियाणि वश्यानि सदश्वा इव सारथेः ॥१।३।६॥

The one who is learned and keeps his mind always under control, his senses are subjugated by him, just like the well-trained horses of a (expert) charioteer.

We usually underestimate the control required over the mind in order to attain knowledge. On the one hand, we can see the illiterate having this one major flaw – an inability to focus the mind on any subject for a reasonable length of time; on the other, we can see the great scientists who have this distinguishing quality that they can focus their mind to the exclusion of everything else. Control of the mind and subjugation of the senses go hand in hand – the more we take care of one, the more the other gets taken care of. However, the mind is of greater importance than the senses and one must put in greater effort to train that.

The sage describes the consequence of lack of self-control –

यस्त्वविज्ञानवान् भवत्यमनस्कः सदाशुचिः ।
न स तत्पदमाप्रोति सँसारं चाधिगच्छति ॥१।३।७॥

The one who lacks right knowledge, has a wandering mind and is always impure in his/her thoughts and actions, that person does not attain the ultimate goal of Moksha, returning once again to this world (through reincarnation).

The sage clarifies that controlling the mind and senses involves cleansing our thoughts and actions of pettiness and selfishness. Our natural instinct is to work towards our own satisfaction, which essentially means satisfying our senses. In that state, our mind flits from subject to subject, as the senses pull and tug at us. Any barriers that come in our way make us commit sins, either through the mind or the body – we curse the person who stands in our way, or are ready to steal to appease our senses. This behaviour puts Moksha out of our reach and ensures that we will return to this world after death – as humans, if we were not too bad; and worse, if our deeds were worse. This may be called the Law of Reincarnation.

The sage gives the reverse scenario, too –

यस्तु विज्ञानवान् भवति समनस्कः सदा शुचिः ।
स तु तत्पदमाप्नोति यस्माद्भूयो न जायते ॥ १।३।८॥

The one who is learned, has his mind under control and is always pure in mind and deed, that person attains the ultimate state of Moksha, after which one does not take birth again.

To overcome our natural behaviour, driven by our Material body rather than our pure self, the Soul must first endeavour to figure out the path to Moksha and Dharma. This Upanishad indicates part of it, but there are many more details that need to be learnt from the Vedas and other spiritual texts. After imbibing these, one must translate them into one's behaviour and thoughts – another task that seems almost insurmountable! Becoming self-aware is the first step on this demanding path. Once one starts watching oneself, she can slowly clear her physical actions of sin. Controlling the thoughts is a different cup of tea altogether. In the beginning, thoughts seem to come by themselves and seem to be beyond our control. Slowly and steadily, the Soul must learn to redirect them to auspicious subjects. Knowledge is considered a cleanser in this regard, as our thoughts automatically veer towards what we are studying or have studied. We contemplate newly discovered ideas and this stops our mind from indulging in sensory subjects. This same tendency must be exploited when we are tempted by the Material world – we have to force our thoughts into spiritual contemplation even while we are operating as usual in this world. To the external observer, the spiritual seeker will appear no different from a regular person, but the reality is quite different!

The sage describes this state in the next verse –

विज्ञानसारथिर्यस्तु मनःप्रग्रहवान् नरः ।
सोऽध्वनः पारमाप्नोति तद्विष्णोः परमं पदम् ॥ १।३।९ ॥

The person who is like a knowledgeable charioteer and has the mind reined in, he (i.e., that Soul) finds the end of the road, where lies the ultimate abode of the Omnipresent Vishnu.

Here, Vishnu should not be mistaken for the common form that is worshipped in temples. This is a Yaugika usage[27] and is derived from the root Vishl Vyaaptau, i.e., pervading. The Lord is called Vishnu as He pervades the whole Universe. We can see that this meaning, too, is different from the Pauranika concept, which makes this deity the preserver of the Universe. This particular adjective is used here to emphasise that while the Supreme pervades the entire Universe, He is not visible to, nor experienced by, all. It is only in this special unbound state of the Soul that the Lord reveals His glory and the Soul is overcome by His effulgence and power. The Soul experiences a kind of bliss that cannot be described in words...

The sage now delves into the science of the body-Soul connection in the next two verses –

---

27 Refer Introduction, Explanatory Note on Vaidika Words

इन्द्रियेभ्यः परा ह्यर्था अर्थेभ्यश्च परं मनः ।

मनसस्तु परा बुद्धिर्बुद्धेरात्मा महान् परः ॥१।३।१०॥

महतः परमव्यक्तमव्यक्तात् पुरुषः परः ।

पुरुषान्न परं किञ्चित् सा काष्ठा सा परा गतिः ॥१।३।११॥

The objects of the senses are subtler than the senses. The mind is subtler than them. The intellect is finer than the mind. The constituent of the intellect, the transform of Prakrti called Mahat is subtler still. Primordial Matter, Prakrti, known as Avyakta, or indeterminate, is even subtler[28] and the Soul is subtler than Avyakta. Nothing is subtler than the Soul – that is the ultimate, that is the farthest limit.

One should again note the distinction between the mind and the intellect here, as in verse 1|3|3.

Also, note the usage of the word 'Aatmaa' in the second line as 'the soul of Buddhi', i.e., the stuff that Buddhi is made up of. These are the kind of usages that we are not used to today, as they are Yaugika in nature. For this reason, there are a number of misinterpretations of this verse.

The name 'Avyakta' of primordial Matter, Prakrti, is very interesting as it denotes that Matter in that state is not determinate in any way.

By Purusha, both Paramaatmaa and the Jeevaatmaa are referenced, as is evident from the fact that the next verse refers to Paramaatmaa, while the one after that refers to the Jeevaatmaa. Since they are referred to as one here, this can lead to some confusion. However, the two are very often referred to jointly in other ancient texts as well. Brahma is called 'Purusha' as It resides in Its Puri, or city - the Universe. The Soul, too, has a 'city' all to itself – the body. Hence the name.

Also, there are texts that mention that Paramaatmaa is subtler than even the Jeevaatmaa, as this Upanishad, too, had declared

---

28 Refer Introduction, Chart 1.

(verse 1|2|20). This is also logical as Paramaatmaa is all pervading, and anything that pervades another has to be subtler than the latter, just as air pervades most everyday objects, being finer than them. So here, we can include that refinement in understanding as well.

Actually, the senses are subtler than the objects they sense, as other texts corroborate.[29] This makes better sense as it explains why the senses do not sense themselves! However, if we consider 'Artha' to refer to the Panch Tanmaatraas, then this order is feasible.

The seer explains who can find the Lord –

एष सर्वेषु भूतेषु गूढोऽत्मा न प्रकाशते ।
दृश्यते त्वग्र्यया बुद्ध्या सूक्ष्मया सूक्ष्मदर्शिभिः ॥१।३।१२॥

This (Supreme) Soul is hidden in all the objects (in this Universe, but) is not visible. It is seen by the ones that have understood the intricacies of this Universe and by the application of a powerful and sharp intellect.

We often hear people saying that all roads lead to God and there is no right or wrong road. There are others who say that there are two paths – one that relies on knowledge (Jnaanaashrayee Shaakhaa) and another that is purely based on devotion (Premaashrayee Shaakhaa). The verse denounces these alternatives and tells us that there is only way to find God and one's own self – that of true knowledge. All other ways are short cuts for the lazy and they end in ignorance. For example, devoted Bhaktas spend their lifetime feeding, clothing and singing praises of the form of their favourite deity, while the statue does not represent anything even close to God! This can be understood as serving the statue of one of your dear departed every day, thinking that the service is somehow reaching the Soul of that person. If one ponders over this, one will realise that this is but a superstition. Most Indians do not realise

---

29 For example, "...अहङ्कारात् पञ्चतन्मात्राण्युभयमिन्द्रियं तन्मात्रेभ्यः स्थूलभूतानि... ॥साङ्ख्यदरशनम् १।२६॥, i.e., the 5 Tanmaatraas and the two types of senses originate from Ahankaara. From the Tanmaatraas, gross elements arise. This same is depicted in Introduction, Chart 1.

this as they have been performing such rituals for centuries, the Vaidika way of life having been subsumed a long time ago.

Having explained the various components of the body, the seer explains how to use them for self-realisation –

यच्छेद्वाङ्मनसी प्राज्ञस्तद्यच्छेज्ज्ञान आत्मनि ।

ज्ञानमात्मनि महति नियच्छेत् तद्यच्छेच्छान्त आत्मनि ॥ १।३।१३॥

The learned (seeker) should restrain speech (and all other senses) in the mind. Then, he should restrain the mind in the intellect. The intellect should (then) be restrained in the great Soul (one's own). Then, restrain the Soul in the serene Soul (Paramaatmaa).

This is the journey from outside to inside. All our senses are perpetually pointing outwards, as the seer shall point out in 2|1|1. The first course of action is to turn them off, so that we can start sensing our inner selves. The first stop in that journey is the mind – the one that monitors and controls the senses. This can be done well by focusing on our breath and slowly moving the focus further inwards. From the mind, we move inwards into our intellect – the thinking area of our brain. For this, we can focus on a single train of thought. Slowly, we make the 'train' smaller and smaller, till we learn to focus on just one object. From that single-point focus, we will be able to move to subtler forms of Matter. The next stop is the Soul itself, which is far greater than its body in capacity and quality. At this stage, it will automatically start connecting with the Supreme, who is placid as a lake! In this way, the enlightened start tapping into a great reservoir of peace from which it is difficult to take them out by any worldly means.[30]

One may again note that 'Aatmaa' is an adjective used for the intellect and Mahat, too, just as we saw in verse 1|3|10. As before, it is to be interpreted as 'the soul of'.

---

30 This same process is described in greater detail in Patanjali's Yogadarshanam, which is recommended as further reading for those who wish to know more.

उत्तिष्ठत जाग्रत प्राप्य वरान् निबोधत ।
क्षुरस्य धारा निशिता दुरत्यया दुर्गं पथस्तत् कवयो वदन्ति ॥ १।३।१४॥

Arise, awake, seek out great scholars and learn from them (about the Supreme). This path is as difficult to traverse as a sharpened razor's edge – this is what the seers say.

Those who are not on the spiritual path are, in effect, asleep. They have not woken up to what their life is really about. They live it day in and day out, going about the motions as if in a stupor. They need to stop and reflect – this is the seer's strong advice.

Once one wakes up to the fact that there is more to life than mere worldly pleasures, one has to seek out those who have already advanced on this path, as the path is not easy to locate. Amidst the din, finding the right Guru is an arduous task in itself. But that is the first task to be undertaken to set foot firmly on the path. Souls like the Buddha could take up individual journeys, with some help now and then, because they were extremely committed. For most normal persons, it may start off as a fad that fades away at the very first obstacle. For the more committed, a few more obstacles may be required to turn them away. But when there is a Guru, he acts as an anchor that keeps one steadfast through all the ups and downs.

It is a fact of life that the sinful path is easy to follow. In fact, it is a slippery, downward slope that quickly sends the traveller all the way down, from where it is difficult to come back. On the contrary, the spiritual seeker's path is like the upward slope of a glass mountain. Every step is an achievement and earned with great effort. However, it does not guarantee an upward movement, as slipping from the position attained is always a clear and present danger. For this reason, the seeker is called 'Dheera' in spiritual texts, as she has to have great fortitude and patience to continue on the straight and narrow path, that does not allow any deviation.

Here, one can pause and consider again the teachings of some seers in today's times that all paths lead to the Divine. This is contrary to all the teachings transmitted in our ancient texts – the path leading to the Divine is one and is very straight and narrow. Not only that, it cuts the feet that walk on it – like a razor's edge. Continuing to live a comfortable life with all worldly pleasures surrounding you ensures that the Guru can also do the same. That is why modern Gurus do not exhort you to eschew it! Guru after Guru is exposed worldwide enjoying immense luxury and committing grave sins, but the followers are blind to this in their devotion. Beware, lest you become the blind led by the blind!

The seer now details where the path leads –

अशब्दमस्पर्शमरूपमव्ययं
तथारसं नित्यमगन्धवच्च यत् ।
अनाद्यनन्तं महतः परं ध्रुवं
निचाय्य तन्मृत्युमुखात् प्रमुच्यते ॥१।३।१५॥

Knowing that (Supreme), who cannot be heard, cannot be touched, has no form, does not deplete or change in any way, is without any taste, is eternal, is without any smell, is without a beginning or an end, is subtler than Mahat, is unmoving/constant, (the Jeevaatmaa) is released from the jaws of death.

What a beautiful description of the Lord! And so different from the ones we usually encounter!

The Lord is not the object of the senses, which are themselves made up of Matter. Thus, It is without sound, touch, form, taste or smell. This is because It is subtler than the subtlest form of Matter. Because of this nature, it helps a lot to have a Guru in our quest for the Supreme.

Some preach that God splits Itself into two, one form remaining pure, the other forming the rest of the Universe including all the beings in it. The Upanishad denounces this view squarely. It says that the Supreme is without a beginning or an end, and nor does It transform in any way during the process of Creation or otherwise.

How, then, can two types of God – one with Maayaa and one without – be formed? And what is this Maayaa that is different from God and overpowers Its very nature? No, God is Ekrasa – the same everywhere, and Dhruva – constant and unmoving. No change or differentiation or movement can be ascribed to It in any way.

Using the neuter gender for the Divine is common in all ancient Indian texts. In fact, even for the individual Soul. This is because the entity called Aatmaa – whether Param or Jeeva – is devoid of any gender. Gender differentiation is through the bodily organs. They are not part of the Soul. When the masculine or feminine genders are used for these two entities, it is only symbolic – to portray a quality that we associate with a particular gender in this world, or, just for poetic reasons.

Formally closing the dialogue between Yama and Nachiketaa, the Upanishatkaara describes the benefits of following the teaching, i.e., the Phala-shruti –

नाचिकेतमुपाख्यानं मृत्युप्रोक्तँ सनातनम् ।
उक्त्वा श्रुत्वा च मेधावी ब्रह्मलोके महीयते ॥१।३।१६॥

Hearing and (re-)telling this eternal sermon, as told to Nachiketaa and as spoken by Death, the intelligent person attains greatness in the abode of Brahma.

The ancients never said that they are describing something new. They recognised all knowledge to be eternal, only the way of describing it may differ from person to person. Any version that proved to be effective needed to be preserved through re-telling. The Upanishatkaara also follows this tradition and asks the devotee to repeat this scripture to those who follow. He brings out the importance of the teaching as that which takes one to the abode of Brahma through Moksha from the Cycle of Birth and Death.

Continuing the same theme, he says –

य इमं परमं गुह्यं श्रावयेद्ब्रह्मसंसदि ।

प्रयतः श्राद्धकाले वा तदानन्त्याय कल्पते ।

तदानन्त्याय कल्पत इति ॥२।३।१७॥

The one who puts in great effort (to purify oneself with the application of the teachings given herein) and relates this supremely secret knowledge in a forum of Braahmanas, that is, those engaged in the pursuit of Brahma, or while honouring learned guests in good faith, that sermon yields immortality (as Moksha).

The verse lays out the duty of the enlightened – the knowledge they have acquired with tremendous effort on their part should not be kept to themselves; it should immediately be imparted to those who have already purified themselves to some extent and set out on the spiritual path of discovery.

The word 'Shraadha-kaala' should not be construed as 'the time of honouring the manes'. Here, it refers to honouring the learned guests who have come for the express purpose of gaining knowledge from a preceptor. Repeating this knowledge while performing rituals for dead ancestors will be of no good to anybody!

There is a subtle implication that such deep spiritual knowledge is not to be given to one who is not qualified for it. Upanishad after Upanishad, and many other texts as well, warn against giving this knowledge to those who are unworthy. Probably, the Vaidika dictionary, *Yaska's Nirukta*, puts it most eloquently as a verse uttered as if by knowledge personified –

विद्या ह वै ब्राह्मणमाजगाम

गोपाय मा शेवधिष्टेऽहमस्मि ।

असूयकायानृजवेऽयताय

न मा ब्रूया वीर्यवती यथा स्याम् ॥निरुक्तम् २।४॥

Surely, Vidyaa came to the Braahmana and said, 'Protect me because I am your treasure. Do not tell me to those who are critical, or crooked or do not persevere, so that I may become ever greater.'

This teaching may appear too severe in the beginning, but the purport of it is that those who are not worthy of this wisdom will not only not grasp its importance themselves, but they will also put off others who may be inclined towards it. Also, since this knowledge is of the highest order, it requires effort, too, of the greatest magnitude. For this reason, there is no point in wasting one's breath in giving it to a lazy person; that time is better spent giving it to a person who will take it forward. Also, the implication that there is no end to knowledge, that there is always more to be discovered, to be told, is a beautiful hidden message in this verse!

The last quarter of the Upanishadika verse is repeated to mark the end of the chapter.

CHAPTER TWO
God and the Soul

SECTION I: THE NATURE OF GOD

After 'introducing' Brahma in the previous section, the seer moves on to describe It in greater detail for the eager seeker. All three sections of this chapter are full of devotion and ecstasy.

The seer sets out describing the seeker and her difficulty –

पराञ्चि खानि व्यतृणत् स्वयंभूस्-
तस्मात् पराङ्पश्यति नान्तरात्मन् ।
कश्चिद्धीरः प्रत्यगात्मानमैक्ष-
दावृत्तचक्षुरमृतत्वमिच्छन् ॥२।१।१॥

The Lord who manifests without another's help (Swayambhoo) constructed the senses directed outwards. For this reason, the senses see the outside (world) and not the Soul inside. Desirous of attaining immortality (Moksha), the rare steadfast seeker, having closed his eyes (and all other senses along with them), sees the Soul residing inside.

At the beginning of Creation, when the Jeevaatmaas and Prakrti are lying in a stupor, it is the Supreme who 'wakes up' and, without any assistance from any other source, starts the process of Creation. This is the significance of the word 'Swayam+bhoo' or the One who comes into existence on His own. Inherent in this meaning is the fact that He is the force behind everything that is created. Thus, the bodies of beings are His creation, too.

Today many scientists believe that Matter randomly arranged itself into this fantastic creation that is a living being, which till date they themselves, with a superior intelligence at work (compared to the coin-throwing randomness of Nature), have not been able to recreate even in part, what to speak of in totality! However, they have to admit that each part of the body seems to be remarkably suited to its function. The senses are one such mysterious creation that have been so difficult to emulate in the robots of today. The senses serve the purpose of the body-encased Soul, working for its survival and enjoyment. Thus, they point only outwards. They are incapable of seeing what is happening within the body and definitely not the Soul. The word 'Vyatrnat' used by the seer to describe the construction of the senses, originates from the root 'trt' which has been described by Panini to mean violence and disrespect. While here the verb occurs in the sense of 'make, construct', the sense of violence is also inherent in it. Thus, the Lord has turned the senses out with some 'force'. That is why it is so difficult to make them look inside!

On understanding this quirk in the construction of the senses, and believing in the presence of a Soul as mentioned by the Vedas and the preceptors before, the seeker sets out to search for her own true self. The first step in that journey is to master one's senses and switch them off. When the 'light', so to speak, has been switched off, a new world is revealed – that of the self and of Brahma. So blissful is this world that the Yogi never wishes to leave it! This bliss is a foretaste of the bliss of Moksha that shall be attained once the body and all the Material encumbrances it entails are shed.

This is further described by the seer below –

पराचः कामाननुयन्ति बालास्-
ते मृत्योर्यन्ति विततस्य पाशम् ।
अथ धीरा अमृतत्वं विदित्वा
ध्रुवमध्रुवेष्विह न प्रार्थयन्ते ॥२।१।२॥

Those who are childlike run after external desires. They run into the extended trap of Death. On the other hand, the learned know about immortality and do not desire for immortality in the transient (pleasures) of this world.

Ignorance is equated with childishness once again! This is a common metaphor in spiritual texts. Just as a child is yet to learn the ways of this world, so also common people have yet to figure out about the 'other world'. Till they do so, they will keep falling into the trap of the Cycle of Life and Death. And this 'net' of death is vast – all living beings are trapped in it. Rare is the one who escapes!

The wise, however, have realised that everything in this world is transient. Just as an examination in childhood only led to promotion to the next class at the most, so also all limited deeds of this world lead to joys that are limited too. Spiritual training leads to the knowledge that there is an immortal Soul sitting inside the mortal body, which is experiencing this world, but not itself so much. The intelligent start looking for this self, rather than the obvious outward-facing entity. But to seek oneself, one must also look for Brahma, because Brahma is the One who will ultimately lead you there.

The seer elaborates –

येन रूपं रसं गन्धं शब्दान् स्पर्शाश्च मैथुनान् ।
एतेनैव विजानाति किमत्र परिशिष्यते ॥ एतद्वै तत् ॥२।१।३॥

The One through whom form, taste, smell, sound, touch and copulation, by That itself are experienced (by the Soul). What is left out here (to know)?! This is That (which you asked for, Nachiketaa).

O Nachiketaa! The senses experience this world. Yet, something remains unexperienced – the Soul that actually experiences. But more importantly, it is God through whose agency the Soul is given the world and the senses to perceive it by. Once you learn about that Paramaatmaa, there is nothing left to know!

The refrain 'Etadvai Tat' continues in most of the remaining verses of this section and even some of the next. It refers to the question that Nachiketaa asked as his third boon: What remains after death?

The seer continues –

स्वप्रान्तं जागरितान्तं चोभौ येनानुपश्यति ।
महान्तं विभुमात्मानं मत्वा धीरो न शोचति ॥२।१।४॥

By means of Whom one perceives both the sleeping and the waking states, knowing that great pervading Soul (the Supreme), the resolute seer does not grieve.

The wise one knows that the scenes change as one moves from wakefulness to sleep, but the one that is watching them remains the same – that is the Soul that is far greater than the body that it occupies. Though it occupies no space itself, it pervades its entire body by means of Praana, the life-giving force. But even this great Soul is dependent on another force that provides it the means of perception, the intelligence to analyse the perception and the reactions of the brain in order to enjoy these sensory inputs. This Greatest Soul, this Omnipresent Soul is the One that one needs to find. Knowing the love and fairness of this Divinity, it can then rest assured that all is as it should be. The agitated, yearning individual Soul will then find peace at last.

Using many of the terms used in the Vedas, the seer exults –

य इमं मध्वदं वेद आत्मानं जीवमन्तिकात् ।
ईशानं भूतभव्यस्य न ततो विजुगुप्सते ॥ एतद्वै तत् ॥२।१।५॥

The one who knows this Experiencer of bliss, this Soul (of all that exists) and the Lord of the past and the future (as well as the present, by extrapolation), due to the closeness of this Consciousness to the individual Soul, he then does not condemn (this world with all its negative experiences). This is That (Lord you asked about).

'Madhvadam' translates to 'the honey-eater'. Honey, or anything sweet, refers to the bliss that comes of lack of attachment with the Material world. The one who consumes, or experiences that honey is Madhvadam. While the Soul partakes of this honey only after Moksha, God is present in that state all the time.

The Soul should know that the Lord is to be found close to its own self – in fact, within itself. There is no point in searching for Brahma in temples and Teertha-sthalas – He is to be found within.

The Supreme controls Time itself. The Soul, too, is beyond Time, as Time is a Material construct. Knowing this aspect of God, the Soul transcends Time, too, even while still attached to this body. In the final chapter of *Yogadarshanam*, Patanjali instructs the Soul about the properties of Time, as Time is the ultimate barrier to cross before the Supreme can be attained.

Knowing that the Lord determines each and every event in this world, and that He is always present close by to protect it, the Soul discovers that there is nothing that is not as it should be. It stops being judgmental and just submits itself to the Supreme.

The seer further states –

यः पूर्वं तपसो जातमद्भ्यः पूर्वमजायत ।

गुहां प्रविश्य तिष्ठन्तं यो भूतेभिर्व्यपश्यत् ॥ एतद्वै तत् ॥२।१।६॥

The One who manifests Himself in the beginning (of Creation) by His immense power, who is manifest before the ether of the primordial Universe (comes into being) – the seer who sees (that Supreme as) having entered the cave (of the mind) and situated along with the Soul of beings, is the One you were asking about.

'Jaatam' and 'Ajaayata' refer to being born, i.e., taking on a body. That is the way the individual Soul manifests itself in this Material world. However, in the context of God, it refers to the manifestation of God by the Creation of the Universe. But even before the Universe comes into effect, God is the One who 'awakens' first. He then churns Prakrti to yield the 'waters', i.e., the ether that will further transform into all created objects and beings. Only He has the requisite power to generate the Universe and populate it with living beings.

Again, being omnipresent, God does not 'enter' anywhere, as He already exists there. This is a metaphor for us to get a picture of Creation. By this artifice, the seer indicates the place where one has to focus to find Brahma – in the cave of the mind and within the Soul, where no sensation exists from the outer world, where the Soul at last becomes alone with itself and the Lord.

The seer now describes that Power as a Goddess –

या प्राणेन सम्भवत्यदितिर्देवतामयी ।
गुहां प्रविश्य तिष्ठन्तीं या भूतेभिर्व्यजायत ॥ एतद्वै तत् ॥२।१।७॥

That divine, indivisible Goddess who becomes manifest by Praana and who is situated within beings, having entered the cave (of the mind), is manifested (by the seeker). This is That (which you asked about, Nachiketaa).

Calling the Supreme a female, after having called It a male and a neuter earlier, the seer makes it abundantly clear that the gender is a construct for this world. God has no gender – only language imposes one.

The seer also spells out explicitly that the Supreme manifests Herself once Praana, i.e., life is created, for if there is nobody to know, what is there to know?!

The other meaning inherent in the 'manifestation by Praana' is that the practice of Praanaayaama is a must in order to still the mind and perceive the Goddess.

The seer emphasises that the Goddess is to be found in the recesses of the mind, by going beyond the mind. It is then that the seeker 'manifests' Her – is able to witness the Divine directly.

In ecstasy, the seer eulogises the Lord with a Vaidika verse –

अरण्योर्निहितो जातवेदा गर्भ इव सुभृतो गर्भिणीभिः ।
दिवे दिव ईड्यो जागृवद्भिर्हविष्मद्भिर्मनुष्येभिरग्निः ॥¹एतद्वै तत् ॥२।१।८॥

Just like fire is concealed in the two pieces of wood that are used to generate it (Aranis), and the womb is well supported by a pregnant woman, so also is Agni, the enlightener of all knowledge, (hidden in each and every object). He should be worshipped every day by spiritually aware people who perform good deeds including Yajnas, day after day. This is That (which you asked about, Nachiketaa).

In ancient days, two special pieces of wood were used for the generation of fire in India, instead of stones that cavemen are supposed to have used. The lower piece was held stationary and had a circular recess in it. The other piece was held vertically in this hole and moved round and back and forth by means of a string to generate sufficient frictional heat to draw flames.

Here, the term used for fire is 'Jaataveda' which implies that fire or energy is to be found in each and every object in this Universe. This once again highlights the extent of the knowledge that was held by ancient Indians and how they encapsulated it in each and every word and usage. And just as each object holds this energy, so also does each object hold the Supreme!

Ironically, the seer uses this term, usually reserved for the Supreme, to refer to the ordinary fire, while calling the Supreme 'Agni' in the next line! While so many commentators of the Vedas

---

1 Rgveda 3/29/2, Atharvaveda 8/7. The Rgvaidika verse differs only to the extent that 'Subhrto' is read as 'Sudhito' there, leading to no change in meaning. However, both the Vaidika verses also support the meaning of the physical fire and energy.

have defiled the Vaidika word Agni by equating it to the mundane fire, the word is typically used for God as it holds a number of meanings, some of which are: the One that delivers the light of knowledge, the One that manifests Itself before anything else, the One that takes precedence over everything else.

A pregnant woman conceals a child in her womb, while carefully nurturing it. Similarly, God is well concealed in all of Matter, but in His case, He supports the Matter.

The teaching for the spiritually oriented is that it is important to ensure that one is pure in mind and deed at all times. The mind is purified by the contemplation of the Divine, while the deeds are purified by aligning them with spiritual teaching and also, very importantly, by performing fire-sacrifices, as these work for the benefit of Nature and all its residents.

The seer continues in the same refrain –

यतश्चोदेति सूर्योऽस्तं यत्र च गच्छति ।

तं देवाः सर्वे अर्पितास्तदु नात्येति कश्चन ॥[2] एतद्वै तत् ॥२।१।९॥

From where the sun rises and where it sets, to Whom all the divine powers submit, nobody exceeds It. This is That (which should be known).

Because of the prevalence of Pauraanika beliefs today, we understand 'Devas' as divine beings in the shape of humans who live somewhere in higher planes and control the world to a limited extent. These myths are actually derived from Vaidika concepts such as those presented here. In the Vedas, natural forces are often referred to as 'Devas' as their powers are unique and important for the smooth functioning of the world. In this verse, the sun is specifically mentioned, while the other Devas – the five elements, the moon, the stellar region (dyau), sometimes the planets, Indra (thunder and electricity), etc. – are mentioned jointly.

---

2 With some difference, this verse is found in Atharvaveda 10/8/16.

As seen earlier, we have a tendency to see these smoothly functioning powers as self-motivated and tend to forget the Great Power behind them all. The verse serves to remind us that each of these natural, everyday events should recall God to our minds and present evidence of how beautifully He has created this Universe. How amazing must be the One who has created such a wonderful world!

Declaring the unity of God, the seer says –

यदेवेह तदमुत्र यदमुत्र तदन्विह ।
मृत्योः स मृत्युमाप्रोति य इह नानेव पश्यति ॥२।१।१०॥

As It is here (in the current world), so is It there (in the next world/ birth or in the higher plane occupied by those who have achieved salvation); and as It is there, so is It here. The one who sees God as multiple here, he attains death after death.

God is One and must be seen as such. Unfortunately, today Hinduism is disintegrating under the burden of so many gods that they would barely fit on one stage if one so tried! Many preachers claim that everything is one and seeing God as many does not take away anything – all devotion counts with the one God in whatever form we may desire. However, one should realise that **truth is only one** and **worshipping untruth yields only sorrow**. For example, if one decided, with all evidence against it, that the earth was flat, it may work while doing farming, but one will hardly be able to explain night and day, and will always tremble when an eclipse occurs. Similarly, when we wish to pay obeisance to our Guru, would it not be demeaning to put flowers in front of an image that has no resemblance to him whatsoever? It is time that Hinduism gave up Pauraanika myths and took to the real knowledge contained in our ancient texts. Then only can we rid ourselves of our various transgressions and do what is right. The verse emphasises this, saying that if we see many objects of worship in this world, release from the Cycle of Birth and Death is out of the question, and sorrows will follow us at every step.

The seer elaborates –

मनसैवेदमाप्तव्यं नेह नानास्ति किञ्चन ।
मृत्योः स मृत्युं गच्छति य इह नानेव पश्यति ॥२।१।११॥

(That One) is to be attained by the mind. There are not many (gods) here. The one who sees many (gods), he goes from death to death.

While the mind does not provide the last step to achieve the Divine, it is crucial all along the rest of the way. With the mind we gain knowledge of the tools of communication, like Sanskrit, and then through them, about this world, and through both, about the spiritual world.

The above two verses are often used by some to prove that everything in this Universe is but Brahma and there is nothing else. However, one must read the verses carefully. Who has to see Brahma if she is herself Brahma? Who is going to be caught in the snare of Death? Is that Brahma, too? Does the mind have to reach itself? Who is to attain itself through the mind? Actually, these are normal metaphors used in a language which is commonly used by the speakers of that language, e.g., saying 'I am but you' does not denote unity between the speaker and the spoken, but the commonality in their traits. Since Sanskrit is no longer a language easily understood by us, we sometimes read more or less into it than we should…

The seer describes where to look for Brahma through a verse that has rightly become very famous –

अङ्गुष्ठमात्रः पुरुषो मध्य आत्मनि तिष्ठति ।
ईशानो भूतभव्यस्य न ततो विजुगुप्सते ॥[3] एतद्वै तत् ॥२।१।१२॥

---

3 *The second line is almost identical to verse 2/1/5.*

(That) Purusha[4] (Paramaatmaa) is the size of a thumb and sits in the centre of the Soul. He is the Ruler of the past and the future (as well as the present). (Knowing Him) so, one does not disparage anything. Verily, This is That (which you inquired about).

This allegory of a 'thumb' is used often in scriptures, particularly Kathopanishad, to denote the Divine. This is not because God is really the size of a thumb. The seer has already clarified that He is Omnipresent. No, this represents the area in the brain where the Soul is situated. In meditation, one must still the mind and contract one's awareness into this area.[5] Once we are with our Soul, we have to continue the inward journey to see the Supreme. This is the significance of the 'thumb'.

The seer continues –

अङ्गुष्ठमात्रः पुरुषो ज्योतिरिवाधूमकः ।
ईशानो भूतभव्यस्य स एवाद्य स उ श्वः ॥ एतद्वै तत् ॥२।१।१३॥

The thumb-sized Purusha (Paramaatmaa) is like a light without any smoke (i.e., it is pure light devoid of any impurities). He is the Ruler of the past, (present) and future. He is today as He will be tomorrow.

The seer highlights that the God-substance is devoid of any impurity that is here today and gone tomorrow. He always was, is and will remain His pure self, untouched by any other thing or being. Even light available in this world is touched by some darkness – fire has smoke, and the sun and the moon have their spots. But God has no such blemish or impurity (like Maayaa, as some believe) and stays untouched by Time, being its Ruler and Controller.

The seer explains the danger of not seeing the correct picture –

---

4 *Refer to verse 1/3/11 for the meaning of Purusha.*
5 *While nobody has clearly identified it in the Indian tradition, my own studies seem to indicate that this area is the hypothalamus.*

यथोदकं दुर्गे वृष्टं पर्वतेषु विधावति ।
एवं धर्मान् पृथक् पश्यँस्तानेवानुविधावति ॥२।१।१४॥

Just as the rainwater on a mountain flows away in all directions, similarly those who see (different gods with) different qualities, they run after this one or that (never reaching the true Divine).

Either the seer saw people following polytheism in his own time, or his intuition told him that such a time would come when many gods would be worshipped! Whatever the case may be, he squarely denounces the practice and urges the true seeker to understand the real nature of Brahma and not get swayed by one property or the other, assigned to one god or the other.

Today, of course, it is very difficult for us to give up this practice, as it is deeply ingrained in us from childhood. So, like the seer, I can only urge the true seeker to spend time and effort in removing this mental handicap and start afresh with one God who has no Material image, who can *have* no Material image, who has qualities that so far exceed our imagination that we can only comprehend a miniscule part of them, who is one and without a parallel, who is completely different from the weak Soul with so many shortcomings, who is as far removed from the inanimate Matter as cheese from chalk. A seeker who is not able to accept this truth might as well give up and go back home...

The seer urges the seeker to retain his purity –

यथोदकं शुद्धे शुद्धमासिक्तं ताद्गेव भवति ।
एवं मुनेर्विजानत आत्मा भवति गौतम ॥२।१।१५॥

O Gautama (of the clan of Gotama, or the great eulogiser of Brahma)! Just as pure water poured into pure water becomes like that (original water), so also the discerning Soul of the seer (knowing God as explained above) becomes (one with God).

Not only is it important for the seeker to first comprehend God properly in preparation of seeing Him, but she must also purify herself completely. Then only will the pure waters of Brahma accept the waters of her Soul into Its private abode, where the Soul knows no sorrow and is free of all encumbrances.

There seems to be a pun on the word 'Gautama' here, which is why the critical merger with God is not stated explicitly. While the word is in the vocative case, seemingly addressing Nachiketaa (and through him all future seekers as well), it also represents the state achieved by the one who 'merges' with God – she lives in a state of ecstasy that does not stop singing the praises of God. Thus, the word is also to be read in the nominative case.

The 'merging' with God as waters enter others must be understood as finding abode in Him and not as losing one's identity in Him. Again, the concept of everything being composed of a single entity – Brahma – does not have much to support it.

With this ends the first Valli of the Second Adhyaaya, having introduced the seeker to the concept of God and how to attain Him.

Section II: The Soul

In this chapter, the seer sets out to describe the thing closest to us – our Soul. Without understanding ourselves, how can we make any headway in reaching the Divine?

The seer describes the situation of the Soul and how to obtain release –

पुरमेकादशद्वारमजस्यावक्रचेतसः ।
अनुष्ठाय न शोचति विमुक्तश्च विमुच्यते ॥ एतद्वै तत् ॥२।२।१॥

The immortal Soul with a straightforward attitude lives in an abode that has eleven doors. When the Soul performs all its duties appropriately, it does not grieve; instead it becomes liberated and is released (on death).

The abode of the Soul is the body it occupies. This body has 11 openings: two eyes, two ears, two nostrils, one mouth, one anus and one genital, one navel and one Brahmarandhra – the opening in the skull at the top of the head, the anterior fontanelle, which is delicate in newborns, but hardens after some years. The Yogi exits through this orifice while achieving salvation. This abode is called the 'Pura' and the one that resides inside it is called the 'Purusha'.[6]

The Soul is described as 'Aja', the unborn. One should always remember that the Soul is immortal, for there are many now who preach that the Soul is created out of Brahma. Its 'birth' signifies only its association with Matter in the shape of a body.

For the Soul to achieve liberation, it must be Avakrachetaa – without convoluted thinking. It is always seen that evil deeds require a way of thinking that is different from a straightforward approach. One has to think of loopholes and complicated plots in order to subvert the system. The spiritual seeker should stick to the path of truth and keep her thinking simple and straight in every way. She should not look for shortcuts and ways to hoodwink or deceive. For this reason, this path is called 'the straight and narrow' or the Kshurasya Dhaaraa – the razor's edge, as we saw in verse 1|3|14.

There are certain duties and obligations that we inherit with the body. Chief among these are the three debts – the debt of the Guru (Rshi Rna), the debt of Nature (Deva Rna) and the debt of the forefathers (Pitr Rna). The teachers in our life – mother, father, other teachers and most importantly the spiritual Guru – give us knowledge without which our life would be worthless and meaningless. We owe it to our Gurus to continue the tradition by passing on the knowledge. Most importantly, this involves the study and teaching

---

6 *Refer to verse 1|3|11 for more details on Purusha.*

of the Vedas, the highest knowledge of all. Then, Nature nurtures us from conception to death. We owe it to the environment to protect it from pollution and remove the toxins that we generate each day. Most importantly, this requires us to perform daily Yajnas to clean the air, and through it the rainwater, through that the water in the earth, and through that the soil and all that grows upon it. Lastly, our forefathers have borne us and nurtured us. We can repay by continuing the hereditary lineage. It was recognised early on in India that children can be a burden and a chore for many. People can think of avoiding the duty of procreation. Of course, we see the reverse problem in India today, but in developed societies, we do find a tendency to not marry, nor procreate. The Indian tradition urges us to not break the continuity of the family tree.

The one who is able to perform all his duties, becomes free of worldly bondage and becomes Vimukta, or Jeevanmukta, and lives in a state of liberation despite still being trapped in a body. After completing his appointed time, he leaves the body, at his will, through the Brahmarandhra, to enter the abode of Brahma.

The seer now takes the help of a loaded Vaidika verse to further describe the Soul –

हँसः शुचिषद् वसुरन्तरिक्षसद्-
धोता वेदिषदतिथिर्दुरोणसत् ।
नृषद् वरसदृतसद्व्योमसदब्जा
गोजा ऋतजा अद्रिजा ऋतं बृहत् ॥२।२।२॥[7]

The one that moves from one body to another, or, destroys sorrow (Hansa), performs pure deeds or resides in God (Shuchishat), resides in a body (Vasu), stays in the Space of the mind, or, in the physical Space after Moksha (Antarikshasat), performs Yajnas and other noble deeds and accepts the truth (Hotaa), sits on the altar to perform Yajnas or resides

---

7 *This verse is the same as Rgveda 4|40|5, Yajurveda 10|24, 12|14. There it also has alternative meanings of God and the King.*

on non-luminous bodies when embodied (Vedishat), whose coming and going from a body is indefinite (Atithi), stays in a home that protects it in all seasons when embodied (Duronasat), stays in a human form (Nrshat), stays in the company of the learned (Varasat), is bound to the natural order of the Universe (Rtasat), stays inside the Lord (particularly after Moksha) (Vyomasat), which is born of water or the life-breath (Praana) (Abjaa), which is born with senses (Gojaa), which is born according to the natural order (Rtajaa), which is born of clouds (rain is essential for its existence)(Adrijaa), has a definite existence (is not an illusion or 'Maayaa') (Rta), and has great goals in life (Brhat).

This verse is often taken in the sense of Brahma, and, with some difference in the meaning, the adjectives could apply to God as well. However, in this text the context, as is evident from the verse before and after, is that of the individual Soul. Hence, the meaning has been given accordingly.

The meanings are more applicable to the noble Soul, rather than a degenerate one, as the Vaidika verse really sets out an ideal for the Soul to follow.

The principles of reincarnation and of release from that cycle are laid down, as well as some idea of how the latter can be achieved by the performance of sacred duties. What is essential for the body, what controls life has also been indicated.

The next verse describes the location of the Soul in the body –

ऊर्ध्वं प्राणमुन्नयत्यपानं प्रत्यगस्यति ।
मध्ये वामनमासीनं विश्वे देवा उपासते ॥२।२।३॥

(The individual Soul that) resides in the centre (of the brain) as a miniscule being sends the exhalation (Praana) upwards, and the inhalation (Apaana) it throws in the opposite direction, is the one that all the senses (Devas) are controlled by.

The Soul occupies no space as it is not made of Matter. At the same time, it is not like Paramaatmaa that is present everywhere. Thus, the Soul is addressed as a 'Vaamana', or dwarf, here. Even though it is so minute, it still occupies the centre of action and controls the life force, sending it to all organs of the body. All the senses pay obeisance to it. While the senses are capable of attracting the attention of the Soul where they want, the Soul is the one that ultimately decides whether it shall be disturbed by them, or whether it will direct them as it wants. One of the big aims of spiritual texts is to make us aware of this fact and bring the senses completely under our control.

Katha describes the secret of life in the next two verses –

अस्य विस्रंसमानस्य शरीरस्थस्य देहिनः ।

देहाद्विमुच्यमानस्य किमत्र परिशिष्यते ॥ एतद्वै तत् ॥२।२।४॥

On being released from this body, what remains here (in this body) of that embodied Aatmaa which is situated inside the body (as detailed in the previous verse) and has been weakened (due to old age, disesase, etc.)?! This, verily, is that (which you enquired about, Nachiketaa).

When infirmity sets in, the control of the Soul over the body and senses weakens, till finally it cannot support the body at all. It then escapes the body to find another abode. What, then, is left in the dead body? Just the Matter that it is composed of! The life that distinguishes it from other forms of Matter has made good its escape. That which has left the body, that which was not seen entering or leaving the body, that which gave life to the body throughout its tenure, is the one, O Nachiketaa! that you asked me about. It is what you seek. (It has no mass, it occupies no space, it has no form. So how can you perceive it? The seer shall expound later.)

In case some doubts remain, the seer makes his meaning crystal clear –

न प्राणेन नापानेन मर्त्यो जीवति कश्चन ।

इतरेण तु जीवन्ति यस्मिन्नेतावुपाश्रितौ ॥२।२।५॥

No mortal lives due to exhalation (Praana) or inhalation (Apaana), but it lives due to another in whom both these find support.

The breath that is the final proof of life in the body is determined not by the Matter that the body is composed of, but the non-Material Soul that imbues every cell in the body with life. O Nachiketaa! Have no doubt about the existence of that Soul.

Yama declares that he has more to share with Nachiketaa –

हन्त त इदं प्रवक्ष्यामि गुह्यं ब्रह्म सनातनम् ।
यथा च मरणं प्राप्य आत्मा भवति गौतम ॥२।२।६॥

O dear Gautama (of the lineage of Gotama, i.e., Nachiketaa)! (Since you are such an ideal student,) I will tell you this secret, subtle and eternal knowledge (about Brahma and the Soul), by which the Soul continues to exist even after death.

Thus, Yama returns to the original question of Nachiketaa – What survives the body? – but, having established the existence of the Soul, he now discusses the how: How does the Soul survive the body? What happens to it after death? –

योनिमन्ये प्रपद्यन्ते शरीरत्वाय देहिनः ।
स्थाणुमन्येऽनुसंयन्ति यथाकर्म यथाश्रुतम् ॥२।२।७॥

Based on their deeds and based on their knowledge, some of the embodied Souls enter a womb to obtain another body, and others attain a vegetative birth.

This is an extremely clear exposition of the Principle of Reincarnation. While most of us have heard of deeds determining our next birth – where and what creature we will be born as – this verse brings in another angle. The knowledge you acquire during this birth will also determine your fate after death. That is why our seers have always stressed the importance of learning in our lives. If we are learned, we will attain a higher birth than if we have spent our lives, say only building up our bodies – *even when we may have committed sins that would typically push us into lower births.* Thus, we can surmise that knowledge is carried forward into our next birth. We can see this in our daily lives – some people seem to learn some particular subjects much faster than others. We call it a God-gift, but really it is a gift we gave ourselves in our last birth!

Trees and other static life (Sthaavara) are considered lower than the creatures that are mobile (Jangama). The reason is obvious – stationary creatures are at the mercy of Nature and can do very little to improve their lot.[8] Similarly, it is clear from the verse that it was well-recognised by the ancient Indians that wombs led to higher forms of life, because the word 'Yoni' really refers to womb, though it has been used here to indicate all the various birthing mechanisms of non-plant life.

The seer now shifts focus to the One who gives life, the Ultimate Cause –

य एष सुप्तेषु जागर्ति कामं कामं पुरुषो निर्मिमाणः ।

तदेव शुक्रं तद्ब्रह्म तदेवामृतमुच्यते ॥

तस्मिँल्लोकाः श्रिताः सर्वे तदु नात्येति कश्चन । एतद्वै तत् ॥२।२।८॥

The Purusha[9] that wakes among the sleeping, while creating each and every desirable object (for the Soul), It alone is the quick and the pure One (Shukra), It alone is the largest One (Brahma), It alone is said to be truly immortal (Amrta). In that, all the habitable worlds find refuge. None can exceed It. This is That (which should be known).

While the Souls lie sleeping in the stupor of Pralaya, He stays awake and sets Creation into motion, making desirable objects out of Matter for all of them.

It is quick as there is no time lapse between Its wish to

---

accomplish something and Its accomplishment. It is also pure, as It never associates with anything other than Itself.

It is, of course, the largest, Its size exceeding that of the Universe. For this reason, all the objects lie within It, in particular the habitable worlds, as beings are particularly dependent upon It for sustenance.

Nobody and nothing can exceed It in any way. In particular, nothing can break the immutable laws by which It governs the Universe. There are those who believe that miracles reveal Its existence. Actually, the opposite is true. All the laws that make the Universe work like a beautifully crafted machine are evidence of Its presence. Just as a car cannot get created on its own, its various parts serving the purpose for which it is built, similarly, it is absurd to think that such a beautifully crafted Universe could have come to be by itself, without an Intelligent Designer determining each and every part of it!

Creation cannot know who its Creator is unless the Creator tells it about Itself. That is what the Vedas do, and that is what this Upanishad is transmitting.

The teacher describes the omniscience of the Almighty –

अग्निर्यथैको भुवनं प्रविष्टो

रूपं रूपं प्रतिरूपो बभूव ।

एकस्तथा सर्वभूतान्तरात्मा

रूपं रूपं प्रतिरूपो बहिश्च ॥२।२।९॥

Just as one energy (Agni) is present in this world in each and every form, taking the shape of the object's form, so also One (Brahma) exists inside each and every created object, taking on the form of each of them, and also exists outside (those objects).

In this verse, 'Agni' refers to energy, the energy that permeates each and every object in the Universe, from the minute atom to the gigantic galaxies and to the empty space in between. This Agni is present in the object without making its presence felt ostensibly. It also mutates into different forms of energy based on the object and its state. Yet, it can be detected when you know what to look for.

Similarly, the Supreme exists in each and every object, without being perceptible to the senses. It differs from Agni in that It exists even outside Matter. Similarly, It permeates the Soul through and through, without making Its presence felt in any way. Only the wise are able to open another set of senses, as it were, and 'see' the Divine.

The teacher builds on the above theme –

वायुर्यथैको भुवनं प्रविष्टो
रूपं रूपं प्रतिरूपो बभूव ।
एकस्तथा सर्वभूतान्तरात्मा
रूपं रूपं प्रतिरूपो बहिश्च ॥२।२।१०॥

Just as the same air (Vaayu) is present in this world in each and every form taking the shape of the object's form, so also One (Brahma) exists inside each and every created object, taking on the form of each of them, and also exists outside (those objects).

This verse is a copy of the previous one, replacing 'Agni' with 'Vaayu'. Vaayu, too, exists in all objects grosser than itself, permeating them through and through. Similarly, God exists in everything inside and out.

The teacher further explains –

सूर्यो यथा सर्वलोकस्य चक्षुर्-
न लिप्यते चाक्षुषैर्बाह्यदोषैः ।
एकस्तथा सर्वभूतान्तरात्मा
न लिप्यते लोकदुःखेन बाह्यः ॥२।२।११॥

Just as the sun is the eye (cause of vision) of the whole world, but does not get tainted by the external defects of the eye, in the same way the One who exists inside each and every created object remains untouched by the external sorrows of the beings.

Without the sun there is no light, and hence, no vision. Thus, the sun is the cause of the eyes. This is metaphorically stated in the verse by calling the sun the 'eye' of the world, the world here signifying the limited area lighted up by it. It has been found that creatures that live in dark realms on this planet are blind, unless they take up the onerous task of generating light themselves! Even though the sun is the cause of the eye, the defects that may be found in the eye, like blindness, redness, etc., do not touch the sun. In fact, the sun never touches the eye at all, whether defective or not. Thus, very beautifully, the seer puts across the concept of how something can be the cause of another and yet remain completely separate from it.

The relationship between the omniscient Almighty and the Universe He has created is similar – He exists inside and outside of beings, but remains untouched by them, their attachments, their deeds and their consequent sorrows. This verse again clarifies that God never attaches Himself to Matter by taking an Avataara. He always remains in His pristine form. Also, the adjective 'One' should never be forgotten – there is no other equal, similar or in any other way comparable to Him.

The following beautiful verse is worth chanting every day –

एको वशी सर्वभूतान्तरात्मा

एकं रूपं बहुधा यः करोति ।

तमात्मस्थं येऽनुपश्यन्ति धीरास्-

तेषां सुखं शाश्वतं नेतरेषाम् ॥२।२।१२॥[10]

The One who has everything under His control, who exists inside all

---

10 *This verse is similar to Shwetaashwatara Upanishad, verse 6|12.*

created beings, and who makes many (forms) out of one single form, those steadfast ones who see that One in meditation, they partake of eternal bliss, not the others.

Primordial Nature is a single entity at the beginning of Creation. At that time, it has three separate properties – Sat (represented by attractive forces), Raja (represented by neutral forces) and Tama (represented by repulsive forces)[11] – in equal proportion. At the time of the Big Bang, God sets actions into motion that later lead to the creation of all that we see around us. This is what is meant by the phrase 'makes many out of one form'.

The 'Anu' in 'Anupashyanti' indicates that the Dheeras see Him only after some activity. This activity is that of sense-control, followed by mind-control, followed by meditation. The first two purify our being by removing attachments from worldly belongings. Once the attachment is shed, the mind is easily stilled. With that stilling of the mind, the Soul that is usually hidden behind its persistent chatter now becomes visible. Residing in one's true self, the gates are then opened to observe that which lies inside the Soul – the Supreme!

In the same vein, the seer says –

नित्यो नित्यानां चेतनश्चेतनाना-
मेको बहूनां यो विदधाति कामान् ।
तमात्मस्थं येऽनुपश्यन्ति धीरास्-
तेषां शान्तिः शाश्वती नेतरेषाम् ॥२।२।१३॥[12]

He is the most eternal of the eternities and the most animate of the animated. He is the One who fulfils the desires of many. The steadfast seers who see Him inside themselves in deep meditation, they find eternal peace, not the others.

---

11 प्रीत्यप्रीतिविषादाद्यैर्गुणानाम् ... ॥साङ्ख्यदर्शनम् १।१२॥
12 *The first two lines of this verse are the same as Shwetaashwatara Upanishad, 6|13, while the next two resemble the previous verse here.*

As we have seen earlier, there are three entities in this Universe that are eternal – Paramaatmaa, Jeevaatmaa and Prakrti.[13] While all these eternities are equal in their infinitude, God is superior as He undergoes no transformation or change in qualities at any time, while the other two do.

The Souls are also conscious entities like God, yet their consciousness is far inferior to God's as they spend a fair portion of their existence in unconsciousness, either while asleep in a body or at the end of the Universe. Even when awake and fully conscious, their consciousness is extremely limited in scope and range, whereas God's consciousness ranges over everything at all times.

Just seeing this superlatively exquisite Being in oneself, one surpasses sorrow and agitation. Eternal peace descends on this blessed person in the form of impending Moksha.

Nachiketaa is overawed by Yama's description and expresses his eagerness to know this superlative Brahma –

तदेतदिति मन्यन्तेऽनिर्देश्यं परमं सुखम् ।

कथं नु तद्विजानीयां किमु भाति विभाति वा ॥२।२।१४॥

That greatest bliss (that you just described), it is considered indescribable (by seers). How can That (Brahma) be known – does He shine on His own, or does He have to be discovered in the light of another?

In a dark room, a lamp is required to see the objects inside. In the mind, do we, too, need a 'lamp' to see the Almighty, or will He shine on His own, like the Sun? What effort do I need to make and in which direction in order to see this awesome Being? These are the questions that arise in Nachiketaa's mind.

Yama replies in the most poetic of ways by a verse that will surely touch any devotee's soul –

---

13 *See Introduction, point 1.*

न तत्र सूर्यो भाति न चन्द्रतारकं
नेमा विद्युतो भान्ति कुतोऽयमग्निः ।
तमेव भान्तमनुभाति सर्वं
तस्य भासा सर्वमिदं विभाति ॥२।२।१५॥[14]

(Where the Lord is,) there no Sun shines, neither do the moon or the stars, nor these lightnings, what to speak of this fire?! Everything reflects His light alone; it is His light that illumines everything.

The Lord is seen by the seeker as light – an enormous light that removes the ignorance from her every particle and fills it with bliss. All the lights that we consider great in our daily lives pale in comparison to the light of that Being. That is why He is considered indescribable (Anirdeshya). All metaphors, all analogies fall far short in describing Him. One can only be given a vague sense – just enough to keep one enthused on the long and lonely path!

Thus ends the second section of the second chapter, creating a desire in the seeker to hurry along on the path to the Lord.

Section III: The Tree of the World

This chapter focuses mainly on how to achieve Moksha, the final frontier. For this, the seer sets the stage by describing the world, its control by Brahma and its hooks embedded deep in the Soul, because of which worldly desires are so difficult to overcome. This section contains the most complex teachings.

The first verse uses an intriguing metaphor for the world and the body –

---

14 *This verse is also present in Mundaka Upanishad, 2/2/10, and Shwetaashwatara Upanishad, 6/14.*

ऊर्ध्वमूलोऽवाक्शाख एषोऽश्वत्थः सनातनः ।

तदेव शुक्रं तद्ब्रह्म तदेवामृतमुच्यते ॥

तस्मिँल्लोकाः श्रिताः सर्वे तदु नात्येति कश्चन । एतद्वै तत् ॥२।३।१॥[15]

There exists the eternal Peepul (Ashwattha = Ficus Religiosa) tree that has its roots above and the branches below. It alone is the quick and the pure One (Shukra), It alone is the largest One (Brahma), It alone is said to be truly immortal (Amrta). In that, all the habitable worlds find refuge. None can exceed It. This is That (which should be known).

The Peepul tree has been sacred to the Hindus since time immemorial. So, its use as a metaphor seems appropriate. However, the word 'Ashwattha' has great significance – it is split up as 'A+shwa+stha (the last bit becoming 'ttha' on conjoining letters). As such, it means that which does not stay tomorrow, i.e., that which is transient. This beautifully describes the world and the bodies of living beings. However, now there is a contradiction between this transience and the word 'Sanaatana' meaning eternal. So, there are two types of eternity that are recognised in Indian philosophy – that which is eternal because it is never born and never dies, and that which is eternal through flow (Pravaaha). This latter eternity can be understood like the flow of the river – the flow is never the same, yet the river is constant. Similarly, the Universe is born and dies, but the Cycle of Creation and Dissolution is eternal, as is that of re-incarnation of the Soul.

Now, we come to the tougher question of what the analogy itself means. Shankaraacharya has described the Supreme as the root for the Universe, who 'resides' above everything, while the branches represent all the forms that we see around us. Most commentators have followed Shankara. This same metaphor occurs in the *Bhagawad-geetaa*, verse 5|1, where, too, the same meaning has been considered. However, the root, too, has ramifications. So, this deconstruction does not seem complete. In my view, the

---

15 *Other than the first line, this verse is identical to verse 2|2|8 of this same text.*

edges of the Universe are the roots and that is still expanding and creating, while what already lies in the centre is evolving into a great diversity of forms. The edge is connected to the centre by Material connections like the fluid channels in a tree. The edge itself has many ramifications.

In the body, too, the metaphor is appropriate. The brain is the root with many ramifications in terms of neural connections and is situated at the top of the body. The spinal cord forms the trunk and the nerves leaving and entering it form the branches. The nervous system being the most important system in the body, it may be taken to represent the body as a whole.

Both the Universe and the body are creations of the immaculate Supreme, whose attributes you saw earlier, too. O Nachiketaa! He is the One you seek!

The seer further explains the control of the Lord on this world –

यदिदं किं च जगत् सर्वं प्राण एजति निःसृतम् ।

महद्भयं वज्रमुद्यतं य एतद्विदुरमृतास्ते भवन्ति ॥२।३।२॥

Whatever is there in this world is all created (by the Lord) and moves in Praana (the Force behind all the forces that exist in the Universe). This world is like a terrible weapon that is ready to strike. Those who know this, they become immortal.

Just as a feather trembles if kept against the outgoing breath, or Praana, so also this Universe exists in the outgoing breath of the Supreme and trembles at His every command. Thus, the world is like an instrument that the Divine can use at His will to wreak retribution on the evil. The whole world can then rise up against the offender and nothing would be able to protect him/her from the wrath of the Lord.

If one is not able to be devout out of love for the Lord, then one should be so for fear of His power to punish.

This verse shows the other side of God – the side that does not leave any sin unrecompensed.

The seer works on the theme above –

भयादस्याग्निस्तपति भयात् तपति सूर्यः ।

भयादिन्द्रश्च वायुश्च मृत्युर्धावति पञ्चमः ॥२।३।३॥[16]

Due to His fear, the fire burns. Due to His fear, the Sun blazes. Due to His fear, lightning and air (and everything else that exists in the world), and the fifth – Death – run helter-skelter.

The Lord reigns supreme over each and every atom of the Universe. If one has any illusion that they can escape His jurisdiction, this verse perishes the thought – there is nowhere to hide from His justice. Even the body can turn against the Soul to give it untold grief, if the Lord so ordains. Even Death cannot be held at bay.

Those who can see this great Power behind everything in the Universe, see the real truth, and so achieve salvation.

The seer now makes an imposing pronouncement that is quoted till today –

इह चेदशकद्बोद्धुं प्राक् शरीरस्य विस्रसः ।

ततः सर्गेषु लोकेषु शरीरत्वाय कल्पते ॥२।३।४॥

If one is able to know (the Lord) here (in this life) before the body is shed, (then the birth was worthwhile, else) subsequently (after death), one will attain other bodies in the many habitable worlds in the many Creations (this one and future ones).

If not for the love of God, one should try to understand Dharma – the right way to live – and the Lord out of fear. Any which way, it is imperative that one tries one's level best to attain the Lord and

---

16 *A similar verse is found in Taittireeya Upanishad, 2/8.*

achieve salvation in this birth itself, for who knows what will happen in the next birth and thereafter?! Kenopanishad recommends the same course of action, saying that – इह चेद्वेदीदथ सत्यमस्ति न चेदिह वेदीन्महती विनष्टिः... ॥केनोपनिषत् २।५॥– if one comes to know the Lord here (in this birth), then it is well; else it is a great loss of opportunity. The seers are saying this again and again because the human birth is the only one in which salvation is possible. That is why 'Iha' – this birth – is of such paramount importance. The opportunity it provides may not come around for many births after that.

Even animals spend their whole life running after the many delights of this world. If a human is not able to rise above that animal existence, then her whole life will be a waste, a lost opportunity. One must put in the greatest of efforts, to the exclusion of everything else almost, to take up this challenge and find That after finding which, nothing else remains to be found...

While describing the vision of Brahma is difficult to explain to an ordinary mortal, the Upanishatkaara gives as close a picture as possible –

यथादर्शे तथात्मनि यथा स्वप्ने तथा पितृलोके ।
यथाप्सु परीव ददृशे तथा गन्धर्वलोके छायातपयोरिव ब्रह्मलोके ॥२।३।५॥

(One sees Brahma in the following ways:) In deep contemplation, (the Yogi) sees It inside himself as if in a mirror. In Pitrloka, It is seen as if in a dream. In Gandharvaloka, It is seen as if in water. In Brahmaloka, It is seen like sunlight and shadow.

The Lokas mentioned are usually interpreted in the Pauraanika way, which does not give a scientific meaning at all. Here, I am giving the Yaugika meaning. Also, one needs to understand that the order in which the Lokas are mentioned is not an ascending order.

The first simile that is given corresponds to the highest state we can achieve in the body – the world of renunciates. With a purified self, we can see Brahma within ourselves as we would in a mirror

– there remains a barrier between Brahma and the Soul, but the vision is clear. This is the state that Saatvika people (those devoted to learning) can potentially achieve.

Pitrloka corresponds to the world of ordinary mortals where being engaged in worldly activities is the preoccupation. This is how our ancestors – the Pitras – engendered us, and this is how the familial line continues into the future. This is the Raajasika way of life (devoted to action and achievement), and when meditation is done in this state, Brahma may be perceived if the Soul is performing Dhaarmika Karmas, but It will be seen only as in a dream – distant and disconnected. Most of us would be able to recall some 'normal' person we know of who has this kind of feeling of closeness to God.

Gandharvas are those involved in fine arts – music, painting, dramaturgy, etc. They are people who are completely immersed in the pleasures of the senses. This is what Gandharvaloka, too, stands for – a world of sensual gratification, a Taamasika world (devoted to laziness and/or sensual pleasures), but redeemed by the fact that it involves great devotion and commitment. Even here, those devoted to their craft can perceive God, but only vaguely, like the moving reflection in water. You may have heard of some musicians saying that their art is their Upaasanaa with God, and they *do* feel a closeness with Him, but this closeness is mediated by something that is far removed from God – Matter in the form of sound or light vibrations. Thus, the sensations one gets are also far removed from Him.

The last metaphor describes Brahmaloka – the world of the Muktaatmaas, those who have achieved salvation and now reside in God. Their perception is without any misconceptions, without any mediation – they see themselves as shadows of the Supreme who appears as pure, blissful light. This is direct perception of the Lord.

The verse thus holds out hope for all of us in that it says that people at all levels of spiritual attainment can hope to see God, however dimly, as long as we devote ourselves to Him. However, the only way to achieve Him properly and completely is to take up the path of renunciation and deep meditation. This will release us from the bondage of a body and give us entry into Brahmaloka where there is only bliss!

Explaining how to transcend sorrow, the seer says –

इन्द्रियाणां पृथग्भावमुदयास्तमयौ च यत् ।
पृथगुत्पद्यमानानां मत्वा धीरो न शोचति ॥२।३।६॥

Understanding the difference (between one's Soul and) the senses that are produced separately, and their (separate) rising and setting, the seer does not grieve.

On deep contemplation, one starts grasping that the senses and their objects are made from different stuff, they exist separately and they perceive separately from one's self. That is, the Soul starts to distinguish between itself and its body, of which the senses, including the mind, are the most important part. The senses are created from Matter, something completely devoid of the Soul, and they may be present in a particular body or not. For example, a blind person has no eyes; a bacteria has the bare minimum of perception. Thus, in different bodies, a different set of senses will arise. The common factor between these various bodies is the Soul that transmigrates among them.

Once one gets this complete realisation – not just an intellectual one but a palpable knowledge of the truth – one realises that all sorrow is linked to the Material body which one takes on as one's own sorrow. It then becomes easy to shed the feeling of union with the body and its sorrows, and become devoid of any grief. Not just grief – one loses what we in the world call 'happiness' too. For the enlightened Souls, even worldly happiness is equivalent to sorrow. As Patanjali says in *Yogadarshanam* – दुःखमेव सर्वं विवेकिनः ॥२।१५॥ – for the discriminating person, everything is sorrow alone. It is when the Soul rejects all inputs from the body that it comes into its own and experiences a state of bliss that words cannot describe!

Describing the relationship between the body and the senses in the next two verses, the seer almost repeats what he had said in 1|3|10-11 –

इन्द्रियेभ्यो परं मनो मनसः सत्त्वमुत्तमम् ।
सत्त्वादधि महानात्मा महतोऽव्यक्तमुत्तमम् ॥२।३।७॥
अव्यक्तात्तु परः पुरुषो व्यापकोऽलिङ्ग एव च ।
यं ज्ञात्वा मुच्यते जन्तुरमृतत्वं च गच्छति ॥२।३।८॥

The mind (Mana) is subtler than the senses (Indriya); the intellect (Sattva/Buddhi) is subtler than the mind; above (subtler than) the intellect is the transform Mahat; and primordial Matter (Avyakta) is even subtler. Knowing the Purusha[17] (Brahma), who is beyond Avyakta, is Omnipresent (Vyaapaka) and without any discernible signs (Alinga), the being is released and attains immortality.[18]

There is nothing substantially new here, over and above what was said in verses 1|3|10-11. The order is repeated to reveal the path the meditator has to take to reach the Supreme – focus the senses into the mind, merge the mind with the Buddhi, meld the Buddhi into Mahat and thence into Avyakta. This opens the doorway to the Lord, the Lord who cannot be detected by the senses at all and who requires the 'inner eye' to perceive.

This point is further emphasised in the next verse –

न सन्दृशे तिष्ठति रूपमस्य
न चक्षुषा पश्यति कश्चनैनम् ।
हृदा मनीषा मनसाभिक्लृप्तो
य एतद्विदुरमृतास्ते भवन्ति ॥२।३।९॥[19]

---

17 *Refer to verse 1|3|11 for the meaning of Purusha.*
18 *See Introduction, Chart 1.*
19 *A very similar verse is found in Shwetaashwatara Upanishad, 4|9.*

The form of This (Alinga Supreme) is not available to direct perception – nobody sees Him with the eyes. A glimpse of Him is to be attained by means of the mind and the intellect that are ensconced in the 'heart', i.e., the brain. Those who know this become immortal.

As the earlier verse had indicated, the meditator must still the mind and the intellect in order to gain a glimpse of the Supreme. Before that, the senses themselves must be subjugated.

This is further clarified in the next verse –

यदा पञ्चावतिष्ठन्ते ज्ञानानि मनसा सह ।
बुद्धिश्च न विचेष्टति तामाहुः परमां गतिम् ॥२।३।१०॥

When the five forms of knowledge (obtained from each of the senses) are stilled along with the mind, and also the intellect no longer moves, then that is called the most elevated state.

In a nutshell, this is what the seeker sets out to attain – disconnection with the body. The intimate connection of the Soul with the body occurs in the intellect, which is itself closely linked to the mind. The mind is hooked up to the senses. The inward progression of the Yogi requires him to move from the outer layers of the body to the inner, stilling each as he passes them. When all connections have been stilled, the true form of the Soul reveals itself, as also the Greater Soul, the Paramaatmaa exposes a small part of Itself, to the ultimate bliss of the Yogi!

The seer elaborates –

तां योगमिति मन्यन्ते स्थिरामिन्द्रियधारणाम् ।
अप्रमत्तस्तदा भवति योगो हि प्रभवाप्ययौ ॥२।३।११॥

That (afore-mentioned) holding still of the senses is considered Yoga (by the enlightened sages), and consists of holding the senses still. Then, (the seeker) becomes undistracted (one-pointed, completely focused). Yoga is, indeed, the revelation of (one's true self) and the dissolution (of its connection with Matter).

How blissful must be the state where our senses do not take us hither and thither! Just as we awaken refreshed from deep sleep that recharges us by putting us in touch with ourselves, how recharged we would feel when we are consciously in touch with ourselves! This is the peak of the glass mountain that the Yogi has been striving to conquer, having slipped and bruised himself so many times in its taking. Patanjali has called Yoga 'योगश्चित्तवृत्तिनिरोधः (योगदर्शनम् १।२)', or the stoppage of all the activities of the brain. What he left unsaid is said here – then, the self rises and asserts itself.

The seer addresses the doubt about God's existence –

नैव वाचा न मनसा प्राप्तुं शक्यो न चक्षुषा ।
अस्तीति ब्रुवतोऽन्यत्र कथं तदुपलभ्यते ॥२।३।१२॥

He is not attainable by speech (or any other organ of action – Karmendriya[20]), nor by the mind, nor by the eye (or any other sense-organ – Jnaanendriya). Other than by saying that It exists, how else is It to be found?!

The Upanishatkaara, Sage Katha, makes it clear that the existence of God cannot be definitively proven by searching this world or listening to sermons. Earlier sages have witnessed Him directly within themselves. They have confirmed what the Vedas say – that God exists and can be found. Other than them, who else can say that He exists?! On the other hand, if one does not believe His existence, how can he ever consider finding Him? This is something in the nature of a warning for those who are adamant that God does not exist. The seer is telling them that you can argue till the cows come home, and you will not be convinced; it is only when you believe that it is possible that you will find Him.

---

20 Refer Introduction, Chart 1.

There is a story about Swamee Dayaananda Saraswatee, the founder of the Arya Samaj, that one Munshi Rama Vij, a confirmed atheist, attended Swaamiji's sermons and was very impressed by his erudition and the scientific nature of his discourses. He had long discussions with him after the sermon putting forward his own contrarian beliefs. He was defeated each time. Finally, he told Swaamiji that you may have defeated me, but you have not convinced me of the existence of God, to which Swaamiji replied, 'No, I cannot convince you, for that happens only by the grace of God.' He later became a devotee of Swamee Dayaananda and devoted his entire life to the propagation of the Rshi's ideals.

This is the essence of this verse. Even though this may seem like a chicken-and-egg problem, it has to be accepted that the belief has to come before the experience. This is something like accepting that the earth is spherical even though one has never oneself found it to be so – one just has to believe those who know better! This is called Shraddhaa.

The seer continues –

अस्तीत्येवोपलब्धव्यस्तत्त्वभावेन चोभयोः ।
अस्तीत्येवोपलब्धस्य तत्त्वभावः प्रसीदति ॥२।३।१३॥

Of the two (i.e., the believer and the non-believer), (the one who believes) God exists, (for her) alone is God achievable as He is, in His true form. (The one who finds) He exists, the direct perception (of God) delights her.

The seer first emphasises the teaching of the last verse – only when you sincerely believe in the existence of God can you ever even hope to attain a glimpse of Him. He is unachievable by the doubting Soul.

However, just believing in God's existence, of course, in not sufficient, even though it is a necessary condition. After much effort and self-control, when the seeker does see God as He truly is, and not as a painting or a sculpture or some such image, she will be so overwhelmed with the vision that nothing else in this world will ever have any importance after that!

The seer emphasises this last point –

यदा सर्वे प्रमुच्यन्ते कामा येऽस्य हृदि श्रिताः ।
अथ मर्त्योऽमृतो भवत्यत्र ब्रह्म समश्नुते ॥२।३।१४॥

When all the desires located in this person's (the above-mentioned seer's) heart/mind leave (him), then the mortal becomes immortal and attains Brahma here.

This statement often confuses the seeker – do I get rid of desires first? Or will the desires fall off after enlightenment? Actually, both statements are true in their own way. The seeker has to give up worldly desires and take the path of Sanyaasa to attain God. However, as hard as he may try, some desires will continue to be with him – if nothing else, then the desire to find God. For this, he will roam far and wide to find the right Guru, the right knowledge, the right path to enlightenment. Even this yearning will leave him when he finds God. Like a contented person, he will then just turn inwards and leave this world to its own devices.

The seer further elaborates –

यदा सर्वे प्रभिद्यन्ते हृदयस्येह ग्रन्थयः ।
अथ मर्त्योऽमृतो भवत्येतावद्ध्यनुशासनम्[21] ॥२।३।१५॥

In this world, when all the knots of the heart (mind) are cut asunder, then the mortal becomes immortal. This is all the teaching (in a nutshell).

---

21 Another version exists here: भवत्येतावदनुशासनम् instead of the above. The above just puts more emphasis on the last statement.

What is left unsaid in this verse is what follows from the previous verse – when the Lord is seen, all the doubts – the knots of our mind – just dissolve. All questions are answered, all goals are achieved, all desires are sated – all at once! There is nothing left to be said, to be done, to be achieved. The Ultimate is in our grasp!

As we have seen many times earlier, the heart here means the mind. The mind is the root of most of our problems!

The enlightened Yogi is now ready to depart from the body –

शतं चैका च हृदयस्य नाड्यस्-
तासां मूर्धानमभिनिःसृतैका ।
तयोर्ध्वमायन्नमृतत्वमेति
विष्वङ्ङन्या उत्क्रमणे भवन्ति ॥२।३।१६॥

The heart has a hundred-and-one vessels (emanating from it). Of these, one goes to the very top of the head. By means of that, (the Yogi) rises up and attains immortality (Moksha); the other vessels go in all kinds of directions at the time of death (i.e., the Soul takes one of the other vessels to depart).

Here, the heart does mean the heart and our ancient seers knew the exact count of the number of larger vessels that arise from the one main aorta. One of these rises all the way to the top of the skull.[22] The enlightened Yogi's Soul has full command over itself and wends its way along this vessel to escape the body in the attainment of Moksha.

The plight of lesser Souls is also described – those that are to take up other bodies after this one. They leave from other blood vessels and orifices of the body. There seems to be also a suggestion here

---

22 *In my extremely limited study of the human anatomy, it appears to me this artery is the one that arises from the Brachiocephalic Trunk, splits into the Right Common Carotid, which further branches into the Right External Carotid. This heads right for the top of the skull. Perhaps this is the artery being referred to here. Also, as seen earlier, a Brahmarandhra is mentioned – the hole of Brahma, or anterior fontanelle, which lies at the top of the skull. The Yogi's Soul is supposed to leave the body through this area.*

that the particular orifice from which one escapes is determined by the birth that one is destined for.

The seer gives detailed instructions to the enlightened Soul on how to exit the body – not that that Soul will need it, but more as an encouragement to the Mumukshus, those desirous of Moksha, to continue the difficult journey –

अङ्गुष्ठमात्रः पुरुषोऽन्तरात्मा
सदा जनानां हृदये सन्निविष्टः ।23
तं स्वाच्छरीरात् प्रवृहेन्मुञ्जादिवेषीकां धैर्येण
तं विद्याच्छुक्रममृतं विद्याच्छुक्रममृतमिति ॥२।३।१७॥

The Soul that lies ensconced in the body occupying a space but the size of a thumb-tip, is always embedded in the hearts of beings. (The departing Yogi) should carefully remove itself from its body, like removing the central vein of the Munja grass from the leaf. Know that to be the pure, immortal (Soul). (Repetition of the last two words denotes the end of the sermon.)

Now we can clearly see that the epithet 'Agunshthamaatra'– the size of a thumb-tip – that we encountered in 2|1|12 and 13, clearly refers to a physical region of that size in the brain (called the heart here),[24] and not the real size of the Soul, for if the Soul is not Material, how can it occupy any space at all?! The same is true for the adjective 'Purusha' that refers to the Soul situated in the Pura = town/residence that is the body, and not a man.

This verse should leave us in no doubt about the distinctness of the Soul, its body and Brahma, for if the body is also Brahma, why does it have to separate from it? And if the Soul is also Brahma, why does it have to perform these calisthenics to release itself? No, the Soul is very much an entity in itself that is pure and is never born,

---

23 *The first two lines of this verse are the same as Shwetaashwatara Upanishad, 3|13.*
24 *Again, in my very limited understanding of the human anatomy, this area seems to be the hypothalamus to me.*

and never dies. It is as eternal as Brahma Itself.

Only the truth can lead one to Moksha. Accepting the truth is of primary importance in this journey, however far that truth may be from our own preconceived notions.

The seer wraps up the Upanishad by closing the frame, the fictional story, that he had created –

मृत्युप्रोक्तां नचिकेतोऽथ लब्ध्वा

विद्यामेतां योगविधिं च कृत्स्नम् ।

ब्रह्मप्राप्तो विरजोऽभूद्विमृत्यु-

रन्योऽप्येवं यो विदध्यात्ममेव ॥२।३।१८॥

Nachiketaa, having grasped this knowledge and the entire process of Yoga as taught by Mrtyu (Yama), attained Brahma and became devoid of Material longings. Anyone who comes to know (Brahma) in this way of spiritual learning (Adhyaatma), will also surely become devoid of Death.

This is the seer's blessing to the reader that surely, if you persevere, you will attain that knowledge and you will then attain Brahma, the Ultimate Goal.

May peace reign within us and in the world around us!

May we gain enlightenment at the earliest!

Uttara Nerurkar is a B.Tech. in Chemical Engineering from the Indian Institute of Technology, Kanpur. She worked for 15 years in leading chemical engineering and software companies. Her last stint was at Infosys Limited, where she worked for over eight years. In her role as a software researcher there, she co-authored a book on software engineering for Tata McGraw Hill. Her research papers were published in international software magazines and journals, such as *Dr. Dobb's Journal* and *IEEE Software Journal*, and presented at international conferences.

Since 2001, Uttara has been pursuing the path of Adhyaatma and studying the Vedas, Upanishads, Darshan Shaastras and other Indian philosophical treatises, along with Sanskrit. She has studied at the feet of Swami Brahmadevaji, Smt. Amrutvarshini Bhatt, Acharya Anandprakash, Acharya Satyananda Vedavageesh,

Smt. Pushpa Dixit and many other gurus of different schools of thought. Her intensive studies have been recognised by experts. She presented a paper on *Nyayadarshanam*, the ancient Indian text on Logic and Reasoning, at the prestigious 16th World Sanskrit Conference, Bangkok, 2015. Another of her papers on the same text was published in the *Journal of the Indian Council of Philosophical Research,* India's foremost philosophy journal. She has presented her studies on ancient Indian philosophical texts in many other national and international conferences. Her most recent book, *The Causeless Cause: The Eternal Wisdom of Shwetaashwatara Upanishad*, has been well received. She regularly writes in renowned Vaidika magazines like *Dayanand Sandesh*, Vedavaani, and gives discourses on Vaidika subjects in various community forums. She has been teaching Indian spiritual and philosophical texts such as the Upanishads, *Yogadarshana*, *Manusmrti*, the *Bhagawad-geeta*, as also Sanskrit, for more than ten years.

Uttara strongly believes that the knowledge contained in our ancient texts is highly relevant today. She is dedicated to spreading this message through lecture-presentations in schools and colleges, speaking at various national and international conferences, and producing videos in English, Hindi and Tamil on YouTube. Her message is to echo the clarion call of Swami Dayanand Saraswati of the Arya Samaj: 'Return to the Vedas.'

Website: http://indianvedas.net/

YouTube: https://www.youtube.com/user/Nerurkar150

Audio of Lectures, e.g., Yogadarshana - https://drive.google.com/ drive/folders/0B-f6xL6_iU7TUjZ2RjhDVFJkLUk